I'm Not Ready

The Realities of Senior Transitions

Avrene L. Brandt, Ph.D.

Science & Humanities Press

Saint Charles Missouri USA

ISBN 9781596300941

LCCN 2015940316

Science & Humanities Press

Saint Charles Missouri USA

sciencehumanitiespress.com

To my mother who kept all the family histories.

ACKNOWLEDGMENTS

I wish to thank the family members and friends who have always supported me and the many seniors and their families whose stories motivated me to write this book.

A peasant makes his old, feeble father eat out of a small wooden trough apart from the rest of the family. The old man would look toward the table, his eyes full of tears.

One day the peasant finds his little son fitting bits of wood together. "What are you doing?" says the father. I am making a bowl for you, for when you get old" says the child.

Straightaway the grandfather is given back his place at the family table.

-A Grimm's Tale

Contents

INTRODUCTION

It's a late afternoon. I pull my car into the circular driveway in front of an assisted living facility. I am to meet a new resident who does not know that she will be moving there.

I have suggested to the family and the administrator to postpone the admission of the resident until I can talk to her a few times and make her feel more comfortable about the needed move.

This is my first client as a geriatric care manager although I have been in private practice as a psychologist for many years and have specialized in geriatrics for the previous fifteen years.

Two days before I had met with the wife and husband about my thoughts regarding the wife's aging mother. "This will work better if your mother is prepared" I said to the wife.

"Not possible" the instant response "It's Tuesday. It has to be Tuesday". They are both adamant. "We made the plans and we can't stand it anymore".

The couple had moved the wife's mother into their house after the local County Office Of Aging found the mother's living situation totally unacceptable- dirt, disorder, and dangerous clutter abounded.

Once at the daughter's house the mother began to complain and be demanding and suspicious. She accused her son-in-law of stealing a thousand dollars from her. Despite trying and trying to reason with her, eventually to appease her, he gave her a thousand dollars. Still she complained and made their lives unbearable.

The time neared 4 p.m. A full sized black car was parked in the driveway of the assisted living facility. An aide, half in, half out of the car, was visibly talking to someone (likely my patient to be).

Then sure enough "Dr. B.... we are so glad you are here. She won't get out the car". No cajoling and no pulling her out of the car. (Pennsylvania has strong laws about elder abuse).

There had actually been two prior hours of cajoling, pleading, logical explanations, and likely threatening, but the elderly mother never got out of car.

I opened the door to the car. My plan was to present myself as an advocate for both the mother's feelings as well as for what was best for her. I did and said all I could, but eventually the couple drove home with the mother still in the car.

There are, as you will see, only two possible outcomes. Either you grow old or you don't. This simple fact is a reality check because we are typically not ready for either outcome.

Unless you are confronted with your own imminent death, someone else's death or aging, or the care of someone who is very old or dying, your thoughts will likely gravitate to the mundane or whatever is imminent. Death or aging (like war or cancer) is not real until it is in your face.

It is then that you say "I'm Not Ready".

I'm not ready to leave my home.

I'm not ready for people to think I'm old because I don't remember a word or name quickly.

2

I'm not ready for my family to handle my money and know more about my finances than I do.

Or to live in a facility where I wait for a second cup of coffee, which likely will arrive cold.

I am not ready to share my living space with a stranger who goes to sleep early and plays her TV loud.

Or to be told I have misplaced something in my room when I know someone stole it from me.

I am not ready to have a bath on Tuesday or Friday or whenever it is convenient for the staff.

Looking back over time, we see that life is always changing. Sometimes slowly, sometimes dramatically, sometimes by choice, and sometimes, just by the natural course of events. Major changes are called life transitions – childhood, adolescence, going to college, marrying, beginning a career, and retiring. These are expected and we plan for them.

In contrast to this, even though we are aware that aging brings changes, we do not expect how difficult some may be. Furthermore, we do not think about them. However, if you live long enough, you will eventually transition into being elderly. This book is written for seniors, for those of us who will become seniors, and for those involved in the care of seniors.

Aging is an underrated challenge. It is the last, perhaps the most controversial stage. Poets, philosophers, anthropologists, biologists, and sociologists are among the people who have offered thoughts about aging. Their attitudes include reverence, tolerance, distain, resignation, respect, and concern, to name a few.

While all life changes have their challenges and turmoil, only for the elderly is there a disparity between the covert and spoken changes. A society's attitude has major implications for seniors' lives. This has been true throughout history. The degree to which a culture values or denigrates their elders determines the treatment of them.

Simone deBeauvoir has written brilliantly about this in her book, "The Coming of Age". She described extremes of societal norms and behaviors. For example, the Eskimo Firewalkers are a practical, but rather, cruel society in the treatment of their elderly. When the member of the group becomes old, and therefore burdensome, they are left on the tundra for wild animals and nature to consume.

Similarly, the Hottentots in Africa, value the knowledge of their elders who preside over the rights of passage and provide the community with cohesiveness. However, when they become physically or cognitively infirm, the son takes them to a remote hut where they receive little food, and either starve to death or are killed by wild animals.

The Chukachee, of Coastal Siberia, however, never disposed of their elders. The father ruled the reindeer herd until he died. He determined land distribution and decided on camp migration, even if he was senile. deBeauvoir asks why this community granted such powers to the elderly. She suggests that perhaps it is because the younger adults could perceive themselves through the eyes of elders who would have been disposed of.

In the Old Testament those persons who had lived a long time were thought to be able to hear the voice of God. They were called elders, or patriarchs, and were the authorities to whom everyone listened.

Seniors in Transition

Psychological Consult

Theresa D. 81-year-old woman, referred for outpatient psychotherapy, due to increasing depression, subsequent to the death of her son from a myocardial infarction. Previous medical history includes breast cancer, hypothyroidism, arthritis, depression, anxiety, osteoporosis and GERD. Medications include Synthroid, Wellbutrin, Paxil, Klonopin, and Prevacid.

The patient has a long history of depression, dating back to an abusive marital relationship. Her previous treatment interventions included anti-depressive medications, a day treatment center, and electrocon- vulsive therapy.

Currently presents as logical, coherent and poised. Expressive and receptive language are within normal limits. No signs of thought disorder. No signs of anxiety. Obvious signs of depression and mood disorder include increased sleep, poor self-esteem, and anhedonia. Memory functions are intact. She related in a verbal, open manner, giving detailed background history, and circumstances under which she had suddenly lost her youngest son. Expresses feelings of guilt for not protecting son from his father's verbal abuse. Husband died four years ago, subsequent to which patient had gone to live with younger son and his family. Cries a lot about younger son. Has problems getting out of bed and, therefore, misses going to day treatment center

Diagnosis: Depressive disorder

Recommendations: Individual psychotherapy, 1x/week.

Psychological Consult

Sophie R., 74-year-old female, with history of frequent falls, which results in it being unsafe to live by herself in the home. Past medical history include, cellulitis, degenerative joint disease, hypotension, reflux, spinal stenosis, depression. Medications include Darvocet, Zoloft, Busbar, Xanax.

Patient has stated that she wants to live with her daughter, but the daughter is not sure they would get along. Also has one son who is not a resource for her. Resident is fearful of falling, feels lonely, but does not want to be in assisted living.

Reports feeling of sadness and depression, especially regarding the loss of her husband. Feels guilty because she was not kind to him, even though he was good to her. Reports family history of depression on maternal side.

Recommendation is made for placement in assisted living for reasons of safety and to alleviate feelings of loneliness.

Diagnosis: *Depressive disorder*

Recommendation: *Individual psychotherapy 1 x a week.*

Psychological Consult

John B., *89-year-old male, admitted 11/20/08, with previous medical history of myocardial infarction, pacemaker, diabetes, degenerative joint disease, and hypertension. Resident is sad and frustrated regarding wife's health. Has had multiple losses. Recently presents with depressive mood. Medications include Percocet for severe joint pain.*

Resident is alert and oriented. Expressive and receptive language are within normal limits. Memory functions are intact. No signs of thought disorder. Resident states he was very happily married to his first wife for 44 years. Has been married to his second wife for 19 years. Had three children, two are now deceased. Has one remaining daughter. Recently relocated due to wife's increasing medical problems. Wife is extremely demanding to the point patient cannot sleep at night.

States both of their families are upset, each blaming the other for his and his wife's money management problems. This increases his stress. Resident presents as conflicted, exhausted, and depressed.

Diagnosis: Depressive disorder

Recommendation: Individual psychotherapy 1x/week.

Chapter 1
TRANSITIONS

There are two general theories about aging. They are the "intrinsic" and the "wear and tear" theories. The intrinsic or, biological clock, theory holds that the aging process is generated from within, based on an individual's DNA codes in all cells of the body. The alternative, "wear and tear" theory of aging, states that extrinsic factors, over time, cause the body to deteriorate from its once strong and viable state. Extrinsic factors which damage the body include illness and external stresses brought about by the individual through damaging behaviors, such as smoking, substance abuse, poor diet, and lack of exercise.

The transition into being an "older person" is not necessarily a matter of physiology. Often it is situationally defined. For Social Security, "older" begins in the 60's when benefits can be collected. For a college professor, it is age 50+, although they can work until they are 70. Supreme Court Justices can work until they die and thus can avoid the "old" label. For the AARP, age 50 qualifies one to be older and for the US Administration on aging, "old age" is 64. The community recognizes senior status with discounts, usually on set days of the week, AARP mailings, discounted meals, and discounted admissions to places and events.

Whichever theory or combination of theories one ascribes to, the way in which people identify themselves as "old" are as varied as the individuals themselves. Generally, the feeling of being useful and having a purpose staves off the feeling of being old. Some seniors maintain excellent cognitive skills while suffering from physical ills. For others, it is the reverse. They are physically sound, but lose their cognitive abilities.

A paradoxical, mind/body interchange also happens as we age. When we are young and healthy, our legs can take us anywhere we want to go. Our senses are primed for learning. But we have less perspective or anticipation of consequences. The meaning of your path is secondary to being, walking, or for some, running on the path. We do not understand the grand scheme of time and consequences well enough to know where we are going, or what will be important. When we are seniors, perhaps the most valuable attribute we have garnered is wisdom. We know what matters, what could have been done, and what should not have been done. We are eager to apply our wisdom, but our body says, "sorry, can't take you there anymore. I'm a little tired".

To summarize life's stages then:

- When you are 20, you have a lot of time. Growing old is simply to too far away to think about.

- When you are 30, you are too busy rushing to get somewhere.

- At 40, you are checking to see what you have gotten and what is left to get.

- When you are 50, you think about where you are and what still needs completing.

- At 60, and especially 70, you say "Time really does fly by."

- When you are 80, you say "I'm Not Ready."

The matters of the senior decades have been described as follows:

- The sixties are a time of drawing back from work and business pursuits, to helping others and looking for meaning in life.

- The seventies bring a refocusing on the family and friendships

- The eighth decade is a time for reflection and seeking inner peace.

- The nineties are spent enjoying people and things on a day to day basis.

It is disquieting for the senior in transition is to see the discrepancy between how he perceives himself and how society sees him. Society expects seniors to decline physically and cognitively, and consequentially in their relevance in the world. The belief is that with age comes decline, disease, and a loss of cognitive ability. In actuality the brain contains trillions of cells, and even a loss of thousands a day would have little effect on the overall capacity of the brain. While some parts of the brain may be more affected by cell loss (as manifested by slower reaction time and a longer time needed to incorporate new information) the senior brain retains the ability to learn and perform the tasks of daily living for a long time. Eventually though, even seniors who are able to grow old well do show signs of change (physically and cognitively) which necessitate a change in life style.

Physical Changes

The physical changes associated with ageing may come on suddenly or gradually. The body becomes more fragile and susceptible to internal and external assaults. If ageing is gradual, there is a slow change in how the body looks and feels. Agility of both movement and thought may slow down so that while the senior is still capable of doing the same things it may take longer. There are also specific changes and losses, physically and cognitively, which can have bearing on the ability to perform routine activates.

There is a common belief that getting old means getting weaker, stiffer, and out of shape. Much of this however is due to inactivity. In reality seniors who exercise at least twice a week stay freer of disabilities, have a better quality of life, increase their strength, are more relaxed, are more independent, and mitigate the progression of chronic illness.

Medical events in the elderly present differently than in younger people. For example, an elderly person having a heart attack may not have chest pain but instead may seem confused. Seniors with infections may look demented due to decreased oxygen to the brain, but may not run a fever. Seniors metabolize medications more slowly so that so that their medications need to be adjusted to avoid side effects. As people age, all their body systems change. The respiratory, digestive, cardiovascular, muscular, nervous system, skin, and senses all manifest the effects of ageing.

Hearing Loss: Some seniors respond to hearing loss with embarrassment. Instead of obtaining a hearing aid, they withdraw socially so as to not have to ask people to repeat things. They may be embarrassed about wearing a hearing aid. They also avoid situations involving conversation. Even after being fitted for a hearing aid, some seniors have difficulty adjusting to it, and therefore do not use it. As a result they forego the use of the device. Realizing this, it is important to get the hearing aid fitted properly and the senior educated on how to use it. This increases the probability of their using it. It is also important to be face to face if there is a hearing loss, and to not cover one's mouth because this removes the visual cue of lip reading. Attention to these seemingly simple adjustments can have major implications for seniors in terms of their staying in touch with their environment.

Visual Loss: Signs of age related visual problems occur as early as the 40s when many people need to be fitted for reading glasses. This is due to an increase in farsightedness. In the sixties it is quite common for vision to become cloudy due to cataracts. Most people who need cataract surgery are surprised at the number of peers who have already had the surgery.

Other visual changes include loss of parts of the visual field often due to macular degeneration, and inability to tolerate glare. Activities such as reading, writing, and watching television may be compromised. Sometimes objects of similar color may seem to blend together. This can present a safety issue if objects are not properly delineated and resulting in an increased risk of fall.

Balance: Problems with balance affect walking and stability. Many medical conditions cause problems with the legs and feet. Neuropathy, arthritis, poor circulation, joint pain, and swollen extremities may compromise walking and stability. Pain and mobility problems can be isolating if a senior is not willing to participate in activities.

Pain medications combined with exercise and therapeutic interventions can help stabilize balance. A cane or walker may also be needed. When a walker is needed it is important that proper instruction is received about its use .It is important to stand straight and not hunch over the walker as this will throw off the center of gravity and increase the risk of fall

Taste: Another sense which changes with age is the sense of taste. Change in taste is due to a decrease in taste buds. This can affect appetite. Decreased appetite may also be caused by change in smell and by dental problems. The taste buds associated with sweetness remain intact a long time and this probably accounts for seniors' preference for sweets. A side effect of diminished sense of taste is weight loss.

Digestive System: Changes in the digestive system are a common problem of ageing and can be an underlying cause of problems with bowel functioning. Constipation usually results from sluggishness of the digestive system. It may also reflect an underlying disease process. Increased fiber and fluid intake help with constipation. Seniors who have problems with incontinence sometimes try to minimize their fluid intake to avoid urinating. There is considerable danger in this. The resulting higher concentration of their urine makes these seniors more susceptible to infections. The use of incontinence products and setting up a schedule for the bathroom can help with incontinence.

Sleep: It is not uncommon for seniors to develop problems with sleep. They may have problems falling and staying asleep and may have disrupted sleep. Sleeping disorders such as sleeping a lot more or a lot less may also be a sign of depression. Medication that helps the senior fall asleep or relieves pain may be indicated if the problem with sleep persists.

Pain: Acute pain is a condition known to many seniors. It may be caused by sudden injury or it may be a warning sing of an underlying physical problem. Chronic pain is a pain that persists for a long time. In seniors it can result from several conditions and illnesses associated with ageing (i.e. back pain, degenerative joint disease, and muscle pain). Seniors can become preoccupied with and debilitated by their pain. Emotionally they manifest frustration, depression, irritability, and anxiety as the quality of their lives diminish.

The experience of pain is very real for seniors, whether or not an underlying cause can be found. Seniors are not malingerers, however depression, fear, and loneliness can be expressed in somatic complaints. While seniors may not ask for help for their pain, this does not mean that they are not in need of relief. Research has shown that pain tolerance does not increase with chronic pain. Instead, the anxiety associated with the anticipation of pain, actually lowers pain tolerance. Research has also shown that chronic pain can cause dramatic changes in the grey matter of the brain in term of shrinkage. It is therefore important to pay attention to chronic pain and make concerted efforts to mitigate it.

The interventions used for pain include palliative medications and activities such as stretching and light exercising to increase mobility and ambulation. Seniors may be resistant to taking pain medications because they worry that they will become dependent on them or think that they will not work when they are needed most. Seniors who believe this or who are stoic about medications should be educated about the facts and benefits of using medications to ease their pain, and how to use pain medications.

In contrast to those seniors who are resistant to taking medication — there are those who (intentionally or unknowingly) take too much or incorrect medications – both prescribed and over the counter. It is not uncommon for a senior to continue on the same dose of a medication that was written for them years before. The body though changes with age. There is some loss of brain cells and a slowing of metabolism so that the effects of certain medications can be magnified. This can create a dangerous situation in that the senior may be taking an unsafe or toxic level of a medication. Confounding this is the fact that as seniors get older, more medications are added to their regimen. This increases the possibility of adverse drug interactions. The use of over the counter drugs and poorly monitored prescription drugs puts seniors at high risk for side effects. Some seniors do not know why they are taking a certain medication and are unaware of the drug interactions and side effects. The amplified effects of medication in the elderly can affect their brain chemistry and interfere with memory and thinking.

Intentional abuse or misuse of drugs in the elderly is an underestimated problem. As with any population the increased dependency on pain medications and sleep medication can have serious consequences. Seniors who knowingly abuse drugs may also abuse alcohol. The underlying cause of substance abuse is chronic pain, depression, loneliness, and physical disability. Some seniors have been using alcohol for a long time, often decades. Sometimes it has been a way of warding off depressions by "self-medicating." With age, alcohol tolerance diminishes, as does tolerance for medication. It is estimated that 5% of the elderly population have abused drugs and 10% have abused alcohol. It is therefore important that a primary care physician monitor medications.

Cognitive Aspects of Ageing

Neurologically the brain is composed of trillions of nerve cells. These cells have an enormous capacity for interconnections.

Learning is the result of repeated stimulation of nerve circuits in the brain. When we take in information, the brain makes connections between nerve cells. Over time these connections form circuits or pathways which become memories. The more something is repeated, the stronger the connection between the cells in the circuit, and the less likely the information is to be forgotten. The number of nerve cells in the brain far exceeds the amount that is used in a lifetime. There are always nerve cells available for new learning – even for individuals who have dementia or who have had a stroke.

With age people can become less active. Consequently there is less stimulation of the brain. Nerve cells then become less active and cognitive functioning slows down. Typically this is manifested in longer times to learn something, or it taking longer to retrieve old information. Memory problems also result from a lack of stimulation in the environment. Research has shown that the brain actually deteriorates with lack of stimulation. Mental activities that exercise the brain can increase the functioning of nerve cells. Thus, the brain can make new connections, work better, and learn better. Using the senses to experience and incorporate new information exercises the brain and increases its efficiency.

Memory: Memory loss is not a natural consequence of ageing but more often reflects an underlying physiological or neurological disease. Families often misunderstand or minimize memory problems in seniors because they note that the senior can remember things from the distant past. In fact, long term memory (or remote memory) remains intact longer and is most resistant to decline than things in the present. Long term memories have been repeated so often that the neural circuits are very strong and resistant to decay. Problems with long term memory are not the typical sign of cognitive impairment. The problem rather is the inability to incorporate new information, to then transfer immediate recall to short term memory, and then finally encode it in long term memory.

The process of leaning begins when a piece of information is held in immediate recall for a few seconds. It is then transferred to short term memory (or working memory) for twenty to thirty seconds, and then encoded into long term memory. The person with a memory disorder cannot transfer information into long term memory. Because the information was never stored, it cannot be retrieved. This is the explanation for the frequently observed symptom of the senior repeatedly asking the same question that was already answered. To be sure, even seniors with memory disorders can learn new things if repeated many times and practiced. Seniors suffering from progressive dementia however eventually totally lose the ability to learn and remember.

Dementia: The cognitive losses associated with dementia are caused by an underlying neurological condition. The most common dementia is Alzheimer's disease, although other neurological diseases, infections, and toxins may also cause dementia. Some psychological conditions (such as depression) may present with symptoms similar to dementia but these conditions are reversible.

The symptoms of dementia include confusion, memory problems, language problems, poor judgment, and a decline on the ability to perform the "Activities of Daily Living."

In the early stages of dementia, individuals are aware of their condition and may become anxious when they find that they cannot remember new information. The fear of losing control and "losing their mind" makes them at risk for depression as well. In the early stages, confusion makes it difficult for the individual to follow through on things they have started. They may have problems with the order and sequence of things and have problems following directions. Expressive language difficulties begin with word finding problems.

The intermediate stage of Alzheimer's is characterized by increasing difficulty with directions, obvious memory problems, disorientation, and increased problems with the Activities of Daily Living. Inappropriate behaviors in social situations may also be evidenced. Typically support and intervention are necessary at this stage and the senior may need to more to a facility.

In the later stages of dementia, disorientation and confusion increase. There is also a loss of ability to recognize people. Problems with fine motor skills and problems with eating and dressing make 24 hour care necessary.

The final stage of Alzheimer's is one of total disability where the person cannot walk or communicate. There may be problems with swallowing and increased susceptibility to infection. Infections, such as pneumonia, are usually the cause of death.

Confusion and Disorientation in the Elderly: Seniors present with confusion and disorientation for a variety of reasons. Rapid onset of confusion (a sudden loss of orientation for time, place, and person) may be associated with an acute physiological event, such as illness, stroke, toxicity, accident, metabolic change, or post-surgery reaction. The senior may be alert but display a variety of symptoms, including distractibility, problems following direction, and problems with comprehension. This type of confusion can be reversible, particularly if it is of sudden onset. The cause of confusion may not necessarily be medical. It is therefore important to examine for possible life events which cause stress, as well as look for a physical basis for the confusion.

Disorientation refers to a person's lack of awareness of person (who they are), place (where they are), and time (what is the month, day, and year). While the causes of disorientation are varied, it is important to recognize that seniors, particularly if they are living in a facility, may have few milestones or cues to differentiate one day from another. Without changes in activities, and with decreased stimulation, they have no anchors to tell them what day it is. They become disoriented because when nothing is happening in their lives they have little recollection of the preceding day. Their disorientation then does not necessarily mean that they have an underlying physical and/or neurological condition.

To help orient the senior it is important to have clocks and calendars in plain sight. Diversity of activity helps differentiate one day from another. Unlike the general population who usually use the weekend as a demarcation point, for the senior (especially in a facility), one day is pretty much like another.

Psychosocial Aspects of Ageing

Psychological and adjustment disorders on the elderly are more frequently underdiagnosed than in the general population. Seniors themselves contribute to this because of the stigma they attach to having psychological problems. This is compounded by an insufficient number of professionals trained in geriatric psychiatry and the seniors' difficulties in getting transportation to therapy sessions.

An unfortunate consequence of the above is that seniors who do not receive care for their psychological problems and social adjustment disorders, actually have poorer health outcomes and are at increased risk for mortality.

There are multiple concerns that confront people as they age. These include concerns about their ability to take care of themselves, and their embarrassment at the thought of being a burden to others. Fear of loss of control, of not having choices, of loss of independence, and of insufficient funds all challenge the senior. What is most upsetting and frightening for seniors is not their fear of death, but of how they will spend their senior years. They worry about illness, social isolation, and the unknown. With age comes a diminished ability to adjust to change. This makes it all the more difficult and anxiety arousing to give up comfortable surroundings and routines.

Grief and Loss: To understand the world of a senior in transition, is to recognize that one of the most distinctive features of ageing is that it is a time of loss. Essentially it is the loss of life as is was known. The most obvious is the loss of friends and family who die or become unavailable due to their distance, and to the senior's lack of mobility. There is also the loss of life as it was known because ageing, as was noted, brings many changes. Physical abilities can be compromised. This in turn affects the senior's ability to function independently, take care of themselves, be mobile, and travel. A serious blow to independence occurs when a senior has to give up the right to drive a car. They then must turn to others to get to appointments, take care of their households, and even get to leisure activities. This also underlies feelings of loss of independence.

Seniors can also lose cognitive abilities which means they have to turn decision making over to others. Sometimes they may have to leave their home, familiar neighborhood, and possessions that they have acquired over a lifetime. In a worst case scenario they may not even be given the opportunity to be part of choosing where they go, or what they will take with them. It is not uncommon for them to be left with the fact that their possessions have either been given away or thrown away.

> *Joseph, an 81 year old retired teacher, moved to an assisted living facility and left his home in the care of his nephew who needed a place to live. He also left his beloved terrier, Buddy, with the nephew because he did not think he could bring Buddy with him.*
>
> *Several weeks later Joseph asked his nephew how Buddy was doing. He sorely missed the dog. The nephew told him that the dog had run away. Joseph was bereft because he found out that the facility would have allowed him to bring Buddy with him.*
>
> *He was lonely, despondent, and he wondered if what his nephew said was true.*

When people relocate, they not only lose their homes but their neighborhoods, places they shopped, their place of worship, their doctors, and their friends. Many of the things they leave behind cannot be replaced.

> *During her move to an assisted living facility, Ellen lost her personal telephone book with the names*

and numbers of her friends and family. At the facility she had a new telephone number but her family had moved her so quickly that most of her friends simply did not know where she was. She felt isolated, frustrated, and lonely.

Lost predisposes seniors to grieve. While some people seem to successfully navigate the grieving process others become anxious and depressed. Particularly in the six month period after the death of a spouse mortality rate for the senior is 70% higher for the senior than in the general population. Complicated grief or bereavement can occur if there were ambivalent feelings about the relationship. The mixed feelings, in complicated grief makes the surviving spouse question the meaning of their life and the reason for living. Grief can last for a long time – months or years, especially if the senior has experienced multiple losses. For a long time it was customary to suggest to a person who had suffered a loss that they "let go" and even move from the house that they had shared with the spouse. But giving up one's home can actually attenuate the grieving process and the working through of loss.

People respond to loss in different ways. Some delay the onset of grief by denying or distancing themselves from their feelings. In this way they try to assure themselves that they are all right and have accepted their loss. Other seniors respond to loss with reactive anxiety and depression. To best help the senior it is important for a professional to distinguish between a grief reaction and clinical depression and/or anxiety.

Depression: Depression, while probably the most common psychological disorder of the elderly, is not a natural consequence of ageing. Rather the loss of sense of self and purpose (which often accompany ageing), in combination with tangible losses, puts the senior at risk for depression. In nursing homes and other facilities, seniors who have several life transitions and losses, can easily become depressed. The incidence of depression in seniors in facilities is significantly higher than in those who are able to remain in their own homes. It has been estimated that up to 50% of seniors in facilities are depressed. Less than half of them receive the treatment they need, primarily because there are not enough trained professionals to diagnose, treat, and provide psychological services to the elderly.

In contrast to depression in the younger population, seniors tend to manifest their depression through somatic complaints, agitation, and memory problems. Weight loss, insomnia, physical pains, anxiety attacks, and irritability, are sign of depression in the elderly. Cognitive functions including memory and thinking can also be compromised.

When a depressed senior becomes withdrawn, they may not be able to incorporate new information. This results in them sometimes being misdiagnosed as having a dementia. In the assessment and treatment of depression it is therefore important that a specialist do a psychiatric evaluation to make a differential diagnosis between depression and dementia. Research has shown that depression can actually lead to changes in the chemistry of the brain. To counter this, a course of antidepressant medication may be needed to restore the chemical balance in the brain.

Certain physical and metabolic changes in the body may present as depression. These include drug interactions, vitamin deficiencies, and hormonal imbalances. Medical conditions such as strokes and cancer can cause damage to certain area of the brain associated with emotions, thus resulting in depressive symptoms.

Depression vs. Dementia: Sometimes depression and dementia do co-exist, but the overlapping of symptoms can also cause one to be mistaken for the other. In making a differential diagnosis, one determining factor is that depression can have a faster onset. Additionally depressed individuals can still incorporate new information. It is their problems with attention that result in their taking a longer time to learn new information.

Anxiety: It is estimated that one third of all seniors experience generalized anxiety. Awareness of the onset of the ageing process may precipitate this. It is not uncommon for seniors to worry about what will happen to them physically and how they will die.

Anxiety is an emotion that can be based on fears that cannot be managed. Fear is a normal response to impending danger. When we are children we turn to adults to allay our fears. Over time we incorporate the calming words of others and learn how to comfort ourselves when we are afraid. Anxiety occurs when there is a fear that cannot be comforted by ourselves or by others. Anxiety disorders are usually long standing and even in the elderly, do not come on suddenly. Anxiety may be associated with medical and/or situational conditions. The fears associated with ageing include concerns about health, finances, and the need to change living arrangements. If seniors have to relocate they may be confused and apprehensive about new routines and about finding their way around. Losing what was familiar to them and feeling awkward around new people also makes them anxious. Anxiety also accompanies feelings of loneliness and lack of support. When anxious, seniors can become demanding, dependent, agitated, and malcontent. When living in a facility they will visit the health center frequently. Anxious seniors can benefit from supportive therapy sessions and psychotropic medications.

Adjustment Disorder: An adjustment disorder is a change in mood or behavior which comes on as a result of a particular stressor (i.e. moving, severe illness, retirement). The disorder is typically manifested within three months after the stress has occurred and usually lasts for up to six months.

The senior with an adjustment disorder can present with anxiety, depression, or both, as well as behavioral disturbance (i.e. aggression, conduct disorders, or a combination of behavioral and emotional disorders). Adjustment disorders respond well to psychological counseling.

Psychosis: Psychosis is typically not a late onset psychiatric disorder. The frequency and severity of symptoms of psychosis actually diminish with age, but withdrawal and isolation increase. Paranoia is the most common form of psychosis in the elderly. While their thoughts are less bizarre than in a younger population, suspiciousness towards caregivers, family, and friends causes them to become more socially isolated.

Psychotic disorders can often be successfully managed with psychotropic medications.

Substance Abuse: Substance abuse, especially alcohol abuse, is frequently under-identified, and under-treated in seniors. Whether they live at home or in a facility, they can find a way to obtain and use mood-altering substances. Lack of awareness of substance abuse means that this serious disorder in seniors is often neglected.

Alcohol, in particular, has long been understood as both an addiction and escape from emotional distress, especially depression. Seniors have the highest incidence of binge drinking. Twenty percent of men and nine percent of woman, between the ages of 50 and 64, indulge in binge drinking.

The danger of health-related incidents is extremely high in seniors due to the combination of alcohol with many prescription medications, such as sleep aids, anti-depressants, and pain killers. In addition, certain medical conditions in seniors (memory loss, stroke, high blood pressure and osteoporosis) may be exacerbated by the use of alcohol.

Suicide: Twenty-five percent of seniors who attempt suicide succeed. This "success" rate is 50% higher than the general population. White widowed males in their eighties have the highest suicide rate. An underlying factor to this is that when elderly men lose their wives they lose their social connections because usually the wives were the initiators of social contacts.

Signs of suicide risk for older adults include:

- Loss of interest in relationships and activities
- The feeling of not having choice or options
- Concern that they are a burden to others
- Loss of interest in the future
- Self-destructive behavior

Risk factors for suicide include being a single male with a history of previous attempts at suicide, suffering from pain, anxiety, depression, schizophrenia, and the availability of weapons.

In facilities (where weapons are not readily available) seniors can passively cause their own demise by purposefully avoiding nourishment. This is called silent suicide. It is a non-violent suicide, caused by resisting medical interventions or starving.

It is interesting to note that more that 65% of successful suicide victims have obtained some type of medical care within the three months preceding their suicide. Seventy-five percent have seen a doctor within one month of their death, and over one-third have been seen by a physician within a week before committing suicide.

Seniors who have not been able to adjust to life changes and for whom the future holds little promise are a high risk group. Their lack of new ideas and interest makes for empty time. Time for depression makes them the highest suicide risk of any age group.

The above points to the importance of being educated about the risk for suicide. It is imperative to ask the senior with signs of depression if they have had thoughts of suicide. The answer will indicate whether intervention in the form of psychotropic medication, psychotherapy, or hospitalization is indicated.

Dependency: Persons who have had to be dependent on someone for a while or have been in the hospital for a while, better understand the complex feelings of not be able to do for oneself.

A dependent senior is indeed grateful for the care they receive but long term dependency can generate feelings of depression, guilt, and resentment. This is especially true if the caregiver presents as if they are making sacrifices or if they are ambivalent about their job.

If seniors were asked what was the most important thing to them it is probable that for many, the ability to live independently would be at the top of the list. Seniors want to be able to live their own lives and make their own decisions. They want to be able to plan this stage of life just as they have planned the preceding ones. They do not want to move to a facility for "old people" where the other residents remind them that they are getting old. They do not want to be at a place where choices and schedules are made for them.

When seniors realize that they cannot totally take care of themselves, they can feel embarrassed. Sometimes they try to hide their limitations, but this puts their safety at risk. One of the conflicts for seniors whose functioning has declined is that they want to maintain their independence, but they also want support. They want to be left alone, but they want to be helped.

Too often the need to depend on others is demoralizing for seniors. Lustebader, in her excellent book *Depending on Kindness: the Dilemma of Dependency*, so clearly states the implications of this condition. "unless we exert control over some aspect of our lives, no matter how mundane or seemingly inconsequential, a significant part of our spirit dies" (p. 126) . The struggle to maintain a balance between accepting help and being in control is complicated. Some seniors, who have made many decisions about their lives, completely give up their independence, lose their sense of purpose, and lose interest in life. In placement they complain they feel like they are doing nothing. Other seniors resist help even though they realize that they cannot be totally independent. They then make some compromise which allows them their dignity.

Seniors who have relocated to a facility find themselves in a situation with restricted choices. They wait for their scheduled shower day, their scheduled meal time, and their scheduled activities. The resident can choose to go to an activity or not but there are only certain activities offered. They can chose from selections on the daily menu but they may not have the food they were used to. Dependency and waiting become closely entwined. The one who waits is relegated to a lesser status which increases the longer they wait.

Without responsibilities or things to do that matter the days are defined by waiting for meals or waiting for the mail. Days without purpose move slowly. Some seniors are tempted to do little, or even to remain in bed. Without landmarks or purpose, one day becomes much like the next.

Living in a facility can cause feelings of loss of choices and loss of control. Loss of control exacerbates the senior's feelings of helplessness and impotence. Research about decision making ability in nursing homes, found that those facilities where residents had more responsibility for their daily decisions, were happier and healthier than if the staff were making most decisions for them.

The relationship between a senior and their caregivers is pivotal to their sense of well- being. The dependency of the senior on caregivers is a major factor in the relationship. Whether living in a facility or living in their homes, seniors can be embarrassed to find that they must depend on others. If the people they depend on present as if they feel put upon or are rude or indifferent, the senior is degraded. What then develops is what psychologists call a "hostile dependency." Hostile, dependent relationships are characterized by anger and resentment. The recipient of the care feels that they are a burden. Having to depend on the caregiver can become aversive. Residents who feel that they cannot assert themselves feel vulnerable. It is a demoralizing situation because they have to depend on someone who is begrudging, negative, or neglectful. It is also demeaning if the caregiver minimizes or makes light of their concerns such as wanting to go home or feeling something of theirs has been stolen. It is hard for a senior to be told what to do, and it is hard for them to ask for help, but it is even more difficult if their wishes and concerns not taken seriously and they still have to depend on the caregiver. Assaults on their self-esteem make seniors reluctant to assert themselves. They feel powerless and they feel like they just have to "accept things." It may be hard to be a caregiver and to see things from a senior's perspective. But caregivers have choice about whether they want to be there. Seniors in facilities do not. Things that seem minor and insignificant to a caregiver may have great importance for senior and may be one of the things over which they still feel they can have some control. Their lives may have narrowed to a great degree and consequently they focus on smaller details. The things they want control over may seem trivial or of no significance to the caregiver, but may matter a great deal to the senior. The senior depends on the caregiver to help with the things that matter to them. Minimizing this makes their dependent situation all the less tolerable.

Those seniors who cope best with dependency are those who have prepared for it and have made choices in advance. Such decisions as to what possessions they would want to keep with them, what doctor they want to be seen by, what medical treatments they will accept, and making advance directives regarding their lives, give them a sense of control. To the extent that seniors make their wishes clear and are involved in their life decisions dependency will be mitigated.

Sense of Purpose:

Joseph, a teacher who had never married, had moved to an assisted living facility, and left his home and his beloved dog behind in the care of his negligent nephew .

In the course of time Joseph met a fellow resident, a blind man, and they began a friendship. Joseph found purpose in the friendship. He felt he had a part in looking after his friend as he wheeled him to the dining room for meals. His mood lifted. That was until the director of the facility determined that he was too involved with his friend. She said that it was unsafe for him to push his friend in the wheelchair so that had to end.

Bereft again, he stopped eating and died a short time later.

Identity Issues: Being designated as senior citizen by the community does not mean that the senior sees himself as such or that the perception of themselves has changed. For the most part a person's identity, their ideas, needs, beliefs, attitudes, attachments, likes, dislikes and so forth remain unchanged throughout adulthood.

Seniors therefore can be taken aback by the way in which society pigeonholes them. This perception of them as being out of date and lacking usefulness is degrading. Seniors' efforts to close the gap between how they see themselves and the feedback they get from the community can be daunting. Maintaining a positive identity in the face of negative feedback is a challenge. Furthermore it can be difficult to hold onto one's identity when so many aspects of one's life are changing.

Even in a more egalitarian society, for men retirement is an especially defining event. A job carries with it a role which is a large part of one's identity. Performance on the job is a source of self-esteem and a way in which people compare themselves with others. Post retirement depression in men is frequently associated with feelings of uselessness and loss of power.

Seniors often have more time on their hands when they retire. When a senior wakes up in the morning and feels they are not needed they gradually lose their sense of being productive members of society. Their sense of value is diminished as this aspect of their identity changes.

An individual's identity is also defined by the relationships and activities in which they are involved. The loss of friends, family members, and social activities, leaves gaps in a senior's life.

Things and possessions also provide a framework for identity. In the course of a lifetime people accumulate many things. Some things have monetary value and some more sentimental, personal value. The need to "scale down" means seniors will have to part with things which over time have become part of them. The more personal the things are the more difficult they to part with, and the more associated with feelings of loss.

In a time of potential "identity crisis" seniors must find new ways of staying connected with what was, and building new connections with what is in the world around them. This means setting new goals, finding a new place in society, and finding new avenues for self-expression. Feelings of being not needed and not useful only contribute to the senior's perception that they are not worthy of love and attention. Seniors then become vulnerable to society's perception of them as powerless and out of touch.

Quotes from seniors in assisted living facilities:

- "It's not my life. This is not where I live. I want to go home."

- "I had no choice. I had to make an adjustment. What choices are left?"

- "There is nothing left for me to do. I wish I would die. It would be OK if I died tomorrow"

Interestingly, purpose can be found in paradoxical situations.

> *Grace, a reserved woman in an assisted living facility, developed liver cancer. Physically compromised, fearful, and limited in what she could do, her sense of purpose was challenged. She had, however a friend, another resident, who took it upon herself to prepare a daily meal of oatmeal which Grace could tolerate. Grace expressed self-deprecating feelings about the need for her friend's help. To the friend it was a gift. The gift of feeling she could help and the gift of giving purpose to her friend.*

Purpose can also be found in returning to a former skill.

> *Giselle, a former hairdresser, was making a poor adjustment to assisted living. Prior to her relocation she and her husband had owned a successful beauty salon where their clientele included several well know Main Line Philadelphia personalities. After her husband died, Giselle move to an assisted living facility where she had nothing to do. She spent most of her time yielding to the irresistible call of the bed.*

> *Her therapist and the director of the facility came up with a plan for Giselle to provide beauty and hair tips to the others residents. Once a week she took two or three of the names on the sign-up sheet and met with them to consult on hair and makeup. The residents loved it. Giselle was delighted and through this her social network grew.*

This is just one example of how creativity can foster a sense of productivity and enhance self-esteem.

Self-Image and Ageing: Seniors are sometimes confronted with people who perceive them to be in decline and increasingly needing help.

In fact, most seniors are vibrant, active, and involved with their community.

So what is it that defines old? A chronological number, a state of mind, the rhythm of your step? Does the checker in the supermarket, who reminds you that you get a discount because it is Tuesday, make you old? Does the 50-year-old, offering you his seat on the bus, make you old? Or being part of your social circle in which your friend's husband has Alzheimer's make you old? Or that an iPad or iPhone are off-putting make you old? Seniors must be careful, less they let these instances define them. They must know when to hold on and when to let go of the past. The attitudes and perceptions of family, physicians, government, private agencies, and the younger generation do not define you. While this is truly a time of change and ageing, the attitudes of a society affect behavior and elicit reactions from the senior.

Friendships: Later in life it is generally difficult for seniors to start new relationships. It is unlikely that a new relationship will have the depth and connection that existed in long term relationships. Seniors need people with whom they can converse about their lives and memories. These reciprocal relationships that seniors had with their friends may be as strong as or even stronger than some family ties.

Relocation and restricted mobility can make it difficult to see old friends. If the senior has relocated to a facility, the schedule of the facility may result in telephone tag for the senior, making it difficult for seniors to catch up with each other. This results in a gradual loss of contact. Forming new friendships takes energy. There is also always the risk of losing again (especially in an ageing population). Nonetheless, even though it is challenging, it is important for seniors to have a social life. This requires that they make extra efforts to explore new activates and new ideas with others. Becoming involved with others has the positive effect of having the senior focus on others rather than being preoccupied with their own life situation. Sharing and helping others gives them a sense of purpose.

In facilities residents can become involved in activities which have a consistent group of members. While these relationships may be less intense and intimate they still provide the opportunity for contact with others. The establishment of relationships in a consistent group may foster the development of friendships which are more than casual. It should be noted though, that activities should be a source of pleasure and stimulation. Bingo is not fun for everyone.

Chapter 2
FAMILY and PROFESSIONAL CAREGIVERS

Theresa's beautiful Main Line home seemed empty since Sal had died. (even though his presence had sometimes been an irritant). She was, at the same time, relieved and sad.

Keeping up the house – the grounds, the bills – was getting too much for her. Uppermost in her family's mind was that Theresa had always been a loving and supportive mother. They decided that it would be best if she moved in with her son and his wife. Theresa thought she would try this for a while, and then return to her home when she was able.

They moved some of her belongings into a spare bedroom which had its own bathroom. Such a small amount of space for her lovely mementos. Her own home was filled with beautiful Venetian and Murano glass from their trips to Italy. Things now unfortunately collecting dust. Her son let her bring a few pieces with her, but only some that could fit on top of her dresser.

Tim's house was always noisy with two teenaged children. Theresa did not feel part of the family conversations at dinner even though Tim tried to include her and was very caring. Every few weeks she would suggest she could go home, but this got no response or approval.

And so it went. Weeks, months. She still struggled with her longstanding depression, but staying there was a practical situation. Until one day at work when Tim suddenly died from a heart attack.

But now, after Tim died, things were different for Theresa. Marilyn, Theresa's daughter-in-law, immersed in her own grief, had little time or interest in Theresa's situation. She was struggling to keep the family business afloat. She worked long hours, was exhausted, and did not feel well. Moreover, she was closed off and indifferent to Theresa. She did not always provide dinners. Sometimes she brought home fast food, or something from the family restaurant business. Sometimes, leftovers or whatever was found in the refrigerator. Theresa plunged into depression and usually stayed in bed all day. She no longer went to the day treatment center and no one tried to encourage her to go. She also became suspicious. She thought Marilyn was mixing up her medications, maybe trying to do her harm. She felt neglected. The vibes between them were not good. Marilyn had no interest in having her stay there, but what was the option? There was now no possibility of Theresa returning to her home. It was a mutually unsatisfactory living arrangement.

Was Marilyn hiding cookies high in the closet where Theresa could not find them? She had only found them one day by chance. Theresa was now seeing a psychotherapist. She liked her therapist. She confided in her. Suspicious thoughts. Unhappy thoughts. Even fear for her safety. And Marilyn was also not doing well... A lump was discovered in her breast.

Birth is the introduction into a family. The life cycle begins with family. The influence of family is fundamental throughout life.

Man has the longest period of dependency of any species in the animal kingdom. Unlike other animals, humans often return to the state of dependency in the senior years.

For most species, the female nurtures her young, weans them, and then sets them free. Sometimes the female and her offspring never see each other again. In contrast, humans maintain very complex, entwined relationships even if the biological parent and child never see each other again after birth. Thoughts, emotions, questions, persist even in the absence of the parent.

Early interactions and attitudes learned from a parent are internalized and are expressed throughout an individual's life. The intricacies of child/parent relationships are continually expressed in a complexity of behaviors, feelings, and attitudes. These complexities affect how adult children interact with their parents, siblings, and spouses, and how they will cope with the parent/child role reversal that develops insidiously as the parent ages.

The past with its memories, conflicts, resentments, expect-ations, indulgences, disappointments, etc., is the foundation for the ability to establish kind and supportive relationships, as well as the negative acting out of unresolved issues. Good family, bad family, tranquil, generous, dysfunctional, supportive, guiding, irrational. We borrow from our family of origin, or react against it, but it shapes our lives, shapes how we form our own family, and affects how we behave with our ageing parents.

Unlike marriage, you do not take vows, you cannot choose your family, and you cannot really divorce them. It is therefore necessary to understand our family relationships. Family is so powerful. More powerful than money, education, sex, or career. The family of origin is basic to one's unfolding life. Humans possess a highly developed cognitive sense, capable of reason, memory, evaluating, comparing, and anticipating. These higher level functions are the foundation for reciprocal nurturance in the family

Despite these cognitive abilities, there are instances when emotions such as emptiness, degradation, and disappointment, are more powerful than logic and thinking. Negative emotions then, can supersede the positive and then can be expressed as neglect, ignorance, and even abuse.

Family Interactions

As seniors age, they continue to have a strong need to remain close and connected to others. Close relationships provide warmth, feelings of being cared about, and enhanced self-esteem. The close relationship seniors have with their adult children and with their grandchildren give them the sense that they are a part of the continuity of the human race. These relationships secure both the senior's place in the family legacy and an appreciation of the knowledge that only they can pass on to future generations.

Seniors take their cues about their self-worth from their family and caregivers. If the people around them feel they are valuable, so will the senior, and their self-esteem will be enhanced. If on the other hand, their knowledge is seen as irrelevant, obsolete, and out-of-touch, this will make the senior feel obsolete.

The mobility of the workforce today contributes to distance between seniors and their families. In previous generations, families lived in the same house, or lived near each other. Families grew up, grew old, and sometimes died in the same house. Parents taught their children to respect their grandparents. In present times, physical distance serves to separates adult children from their ageing parents and from the reality of mortality. It is not uncommon for seniors to suffer this distancing. They experience the distance as their not being useful and valuable. Unfortunately, their sense of being out-of-the-loop, isolated, and irrelevant puts them at risk for depression and health problems.

Lorraine, a rather feisty and sometimes irritable woman, had been at the same assisted living facility for ten years. Despite her tendency to often need help calming down, she was in truth a very resourceful and independent woman who would rely on herself, rather than ask her family for money.

Early on in her stay at the facility, she volunteered her time at a day care center so that she would not be sitting around unproductively in the facility.

As time passed, her finances declined to the point that the family could not afford for her to stay there. She was totally out of financial resources.

The administrator of the facility and all the personnel liked Lorraine and appreciated her specialness. Therefore, the administrator talked with the family and worked it out that Lorraine could stay a bit longer at half the fee. Eventually, when they could no longer do that, they set a time limit where Lorraine could at least stay after the Christmas holidays. Then Lorraine would have to move to a county run facility. This might be disastrous. She would have to share a room with somebody (in fact, she was vulnerable to misunderstandings with other residents). Lorraine loved where she lived, but she had a creative, if somewhat vulgar, humor. However, it resulted in her being fearful that if she did not behave well, she would have to leave. This made her quite receptive to working hard with her therapist to develop coping and problem-solving skills. Thus, she was always learning how to avoid altercations with other residents – a byproduct of living in a small community with residents who themselves had problems and knew a lot about each other.

Ultimately, there came a point where Lorraine had to move as the administrator could no longer absorb the cost of her staying.

The family was reluctant to tell Lorraine this, fearful that she would be upset, depressed, and without the motivation to stay, would regress behaviorally.

As the time of Lorraine's necessary departure approached, the family decided to put off telling her until only one day before. They wanted there to be what they thought would be a shorter period of her being upset.

This actually gave Lorraine little time to pack, say all her goodbyes, or deal with the fact that she was moving from a facility she had called home for ten years to a lesser facility. Families often do not anticipate their loved ones living as long as they do and continuing to need money to live.

Lorraine was told one day before the move.

Families must be advocates for their senior's well-being. Advocacy begins with being in touch with the senior and being sensitive both to their verbalized and unspoken needs. Family contacts and visits serve as an anchor for seniors and assure them that one day is just not like the next. Regular telephone calls keep the senior in the loop, as do including the senior in family events, taking them out to dinner, and taking them to special occasions. Being out with a senior is an opportunity not only to spend time, but to exchange thoughts, feelings, and memories.

Family is more than just immediate members. It is important to understand that keeping the senior in touch with the extended family, with friends, and with the community, also promotes the sense that the senior remains part of the world. Families, who need guidelines for how much contact to have with their senior, should ask themselves how often they would like to be contacted when they are a senior.

Seniors have been noted to say:

- "Yes, my daughter comes to visit. She pays the bills and takes the laundry."

- "My son spends 15 minutes and leaves."

- "My kids take me to doctor's appointments when needed, but they are busy. They have jobs. It's not easy for them."

Families sometimes fail to realize that talking meaningfully with their senior promotes good feelings in both. Contacts filled with silences make for short visits. There is, in reality, so much to talk about with a parent/senior. There are shared memories, family events, and family pictures, sharing a meal, and going to a movie that can be enjoyed together. Just including the senior in your life, talking about your day, and asking for advice, means so much to a senior.

Sometimes families avoid seeing their senior because they feel guilty about placement. They don't want to hear. "I want to go home". "I can't sleep here". Families sense they are out of rationalizations, "Don't you have everything you need?" "Isn't the food good here?" "You know you need a place where you can be safe".

> *Roger*, *a devoted son, became increasingly reluctant to visit his mother in assisted living. She cried. She implored. She bargained. "Just let me come home for a little bit, to sit in the back, and look at the garden."*
>
> *Roger was afraid that if he took her out for the day, he would never be able to get her back to the facility.*

Finally, with the help of the staff, it was agreed that he would take his mother to spend time in her garden if there were no pleas about coming back to the facility. Progress was made because Roger had listened to his mother's wishes and she had listened to his concerns.

Her once a week visit to her garden relieved the strain for both of them.

Sometimes bad luck ends the dream of the senior and makes placement necessary. Many seniors have worked hard all their lives and look forward to retirement. They think, "I'll travel, I'll golf, I'll garden". Then, bad luck.

Elizabeth was just such a person. She worked hard after her husband died, and put her son through medical school. He became a very successful dermatologist.

Just before she was to retire, Elizabeth suffered a stroke which left her wheelchair-bound. Her son visited infrequently. His wife was always too busy, even to bring Elizabeth alternate clothing when the seasons changed. Their infrequent visits were brief. Elizabeth felt she almost had to beg for time, but feared that if she complained, she would alienate her son and get even less attention than she already had to accept.

She never mentioned what she had done for her son, but did suffer the loss of her dreams. She worried about how to navigate the now tenuous relationship with her son and his new wife.

Family Structures

The stability of the family, as well as the parent/child history of interactions, is a good prognosticator of how well the family will adjust when the senior parent needs assistance. If children felt loved and supported, they will likely want to give back to their senior parent. If the relationship was one in which the children felt controlled, criticized, neglected, or overindulged, they will be less likely to be good caregivers for their parents. In addition to the effects of the past relationship, the structure and cohesiveness of the current family has implications of how well the family will interact with an ageing parent.

The cohesive vs. the fragmented family. The fragmented family is one that never worked in a coordinated, organized manner. In contrast, the cohesive family in one in which the family members functioned as a whole and not as isolated individuals. The success of a plan for the senior is largely dependent on how well the family members cooperate in their planning and decision-making. The fragmented family will be in conflict, will not negotiate well, and will not be able to delegate responsibility. In the fragmented family, family members will make unilateral decisions which will result in conflict and poor problem-solving. The one who loses in this scenario is the senior.

The productive vs. the non-productive family. Coordinated planning is necessary when the senior's life must change. The productive family begins by deciding who will be the primary coordinator. This person is able to organize, delegate responsibility, and function effectively. Non-productive families will not be able to make a viable plan with or without input from the senior. Again, the one who loses is the senior.

The fragile vs. the stable family. The stability of the family is a reflection of how well they functioned in previous situations. For example, the child who always needed the parent's approval will have difficulty deciding on something that will displease the parent, even if it is a good decision. A child who felt controlled by the parent may have difficulty being sensitive to the parent. The flexibility of the family and its ability to adapt to change also affects how well the senior will adjust to change. When a senior can no longer be independent, a family's strengths and weaknesses become more obvious. The realization that a senior is in the "last transition", elicits many emotions. Old conflicts, unresolved hurts, unmet needs, as well as fears of loss and abandonment resurface. On a positive note though, this time can be an opportunity to share feelings, resolve issues, and try to have the best possible relationship. Sometimes, especially if the senior lives at a distance, it is tempting to isolate or deny feelings and not stir things up. In reality, though, this time is the last chance to talk with a parent and come to terms with the issues from the past.

The relationship with our parent was our "primary" relationship. As such, it is the prototype for all of our future relationships. We can either reproduce the same type of relationship we had with our parents or bounce off them and form relationships that are dramatically different from what we lived as children. Whichever path we take, our understanding and resolution of issues with our parents is necessary in order to form healthy relationship with others.

Approaching a parent about the past can be painful. The awakening of old hurts and conflicts is something a parent may not want to do. Attempts at resolution should not begin with anger and accusations. Instead, it should start with the explanation that one is trying to express feelings and come to terms with the past – for both of you. Even if a parent resists, you will at least know you tried to get to a better place with them.

It is helpful at these times to accept that some things cannot be changed. Personality, for example, is fixed at a very young age. Who we are – out traits, defenses, and ways of reacting, are formed very early in our lives and become more fixed with time. Because some things cannot change, efforts to resolve old issues may not be what was hoped for.

Nonetheless, the effort to make peace with the past can have a positive impact and facilitate planning with the senior. The lack of resolution of issues sets the stage for both acting out and unhealthy behaviors.

Family Emotions

As a senior's needs develop over time, it is likely that their adult children will experience a wide range of emotions. Adult children can get anxious and stressed as they become aware that their parents are getting older.

In general, it is difficult for both families and ageing seniors to accept that things are changing for the senior. This is more apt to occur if the changes are slow and easy to ignore. Slow change enables denial, and denial prevents families from thinking and planning ahead.

Denial is the most primitive of psychological defenses. It allows us to avoid acknowledging painful realities. On a primitive level, denial protects us from anxiety, pain, and loss. Both seniors and their adult children may initially react to the ageing of a senior with denial. Both may try to minimize the change they see or attribute it to normal ageing. Denial, however, prevents people from assessing and planning for change. Sometimes families who cannot get past denial, need professional intervention to help begin the process of problem-solving.

Adult children are usually busy with their own lives. As they become more involved with the needs of their parents, they may feel pressured and concerned that they will not have the time to take care of their own and their family's needs. Time pressures and feeling that their own lives are becoming restricted, may lead to feelings of resentment and anger.

Resentment. Family members who become caregivers may resent the time they have to give to a needy parent. This is particularly true if the senior is demanding and was not nurturing or supportive of the child when they were young. Not all people have the skill, temperament, and time to be good caregivers. Yet, for some adult children, their becoming the caregiver may be the only option. This sets the stage for a difficult situation.

Anger. Anger is a powerful and unacceptable emotion. Family members, however, may find themselves angry for a variety of reasons. The frustration of caregiving readily leads to anger. Adult children may get frustrated and angry if the senior is uncooperative, demanding, or inappropriate. The loss of parental support can also lead to feelings of loss, resentment, and anger. Feeling pressured, burdened, and unappreciated, also leaves caregivers feeling angry.

Guilt. A common reaction to anger is guilt. Guilt can be an immobilizing emotion. Family members may feel guilty about their thoughts, emotions, behaviors, and wishes. If they feel they are not doing enough, not taking good enough care of the senior, or have not intervened quickly enough, they feel guilty. Adult children may feel guilty about negative behaviors towards the senior, and about conflicts in their relationship with the senior. If they get angry, impatient, or resentful --- guilt. If they want to escape or distance themselves for their ageing parent --- guilt. If they have to make a decision which is in opposition to their parent's wishes, (for example, initiating a move to a facility) ---- guilt. Families must realize that they cannot stop the passage of life. They cannot always control or predict the consequences of their interventions and behaviors. Guilt can, however, interfere with making necessary decisions (Brandt, Caregiver's Reprieve, 1997). When families are making choices for their seniors, thinking ahead, not guilt, should drive their choices.

Many times, families take responsibility for the care of the senior when it is truly beyond their capacity to do so.

> *Marion and her husband had decided to take his father into their home because he could no longer care*

for himself. Arthur was adored by the couple and their adolescent son. He had been a frequent visitor to their house. They thought Arthur would be company for their son when they were out. He was funny and caring.

Arthur was able to move into a separate area of the house with its own bathroom. All went well for a few weeks. Then Arthur began to complain about noise, frequently interjected his opinions about family matters, took his car out and got lost, and had small fender benders. He also began to "miss" the bowl in the bathroom.

Marion, typically soft spoken and kindly, became increasingly frustrated. She got little support from the family and, in fact, other members of the household also became less careful in their toileting.

It was the "misses" in the bathroom that actually brought Marion to the point of emotional decompensation. She sought professional counseling.

Gradually through her sessions, she decided to get a job outside the house, became more assertive, and made it obvious that she was not the maid.

Soon after that, a family conference resulted in the decision that Arthur really needed to move to an assisted living facility.

Families must do what they can do to offer support and care, but must also recognize their limits and not be driven by guilt.

Depression. Family members who are caregivers for an ageing parent are at risk for depression. The incidence of depression in family caregivers is three times higher than in comparable population of non -caregivers. It is depressing for children to see their parents ageing and to experience the change and losses that occur as parents grow older.

Acceptance. Coming to terms with the ageing of a parent occurs when the family realizes that the changes that they are seeing are real. Coming to terms also means that they have worked out their own feelings of anger, fear, and guilt. It is a difficult process to accept that the nature of the relationship with a parent has changed. Acceptance though is a necessary prerequisite for the family working productively in the senior's best interest.

Interventions

The family is pivotal in assisting the senior in their time of transition. They can gather information about resources, be advocates, provide emotional support, and help the senior adjust to change.

Accepting that a senior needs help and must depend on adult children is complicated for all involved. Adult children feel the shift in dependency. Often they cannot depend on their parents as before and must instead take on responsibilities for their parent's financial, physical, and general well-being. This role reversal is embarrassing for both the senior and their family.

No one teaches us how to parent our parents. For seniors, relinquishing decision-making is an affront to their self-esteem. For adult children, it can be embarrassing to see their parents as dependent and vulnerable. This is a sensitive issue and one that can impact on the relationship. It requires insight to know how much to take over and what to leave in the province of the senior. If not handled well, the outcome can be tension, frustration, and resentment between the adult children and the parent they are trying to help. A good rule of thumb is to have seniors do as much for themselves as they can, for as long as they can. Whether a senior ages at home or moves to a facility, changes in physical and cognitive capabilities (even if mild) puts them in a position where others may be making interventions and choices for them.

While necessary, this is a sensitive situation. This is especially true when the senior gives Power of Attorney to someone who is now able to make a variety of decisions without even involving or apprising the senior. For the most part, caregivers intervene honestly, sincerely, and with the senior's best interest at heart. However, when this is not the case, caregivers can be insensitive, and even abusive.

Selena *was always well-groomed, poised, and alert. She had been moved to an assisted living facility by her adopted daughter. The daughter manipulated the move by implying that it was temporary.*

Soon Selena stated that she was unhappy and wanted to go home. As her feelings persisted, she was referred to be seen by a psychologist for depression. She was cognitively clear and physically healthy. Repeatedly, in the course of the weeks, she stated how much she missed her home. She had worked hard all of her life to pay it off and missed her neighbors, friends, and relatives who were nearby. She could not adjust to being in assisted living. Her adopted daughter was evasive – never really explaining to Selena why she needed to be in assisted living or that her stay would be permanent. Selena, in fact, did not know that the daughter had sold her house and possessions and that there was no home to go to. (This is possible when there is a Power of Attorney).

When Selena's therapist suggested a family meeting, the daughter reluctantly agreed. She insisted, though, that Selena not be told about the sale of her house.

The therapist suggested that the daughter bring some of Selena's belongings to personalize her room (bedspreads, curtains, chair, small table), and make is less institutional.

One week later, the therapist was apprised that the daughter decided that Selena would not be seen by the therapist anymore. When the therapist to question this, as it was not Selena's choice, the daughter said she objected to the use of the word "institutional" and unfortunately for Selena, the daughter had Power of Attorney.

For weeks Selena would see her therapist in the hallway, "are you seeing me today?" Next week – "are you seeing me today?"

When a senior gives Power of Attorney, they must understand the implications of this legal arrangement. This is a formal legal intervention which gives someone authority to make decisions for someone else.

Whether at home or in a facility seniors who cannot function independently, may find themselves subject to the decisions of the family.

*Subsequent to the death of her husband and at the suggestion of her step-son, **Jean** relocated to an assisted living facility to the North. She had loved living in Florida and was deeply grieving the loss of her husband and the life they had shared. She was referred to a psychologist for her depression. She used the sessions well and worked on her grief issues. She said that the sessions improved her mood.*

After some time, her step-son came north to visit. He noted that Jean had not remembered some things he had told her. He then determined that she could not possibly remember what was said from one of her therapy sessions to another.

He told the facility nurse that he did not want the psychologist to see his step-mother any longer, even though Jean looked forward to the sessions. The facility complied and the sessions were terminated.

Jean, fearful of alienating her only family member, did not speak up for herself.

In the ensuing weeks, her mood declined, she became less involved in the program, and again presented with depression.

***Martin**, a 75-year-old diabetic, was admitted to a nursing home in eastern Pennsylvania. Martin had lived independently for many years. He liked his home, he loved cooking and seeing his friends. Unfortunately, he had a non-healing wound on his right foot. He was, therefore, admitted to a nursing home. The condition of the foot worsened. He had his right heel amputated. Nonetheless, his mood remained good, because he knew in time he would be able to manage by himself at home.*

Time passed. The wound was not healing well. Martin developed a fever, which left him cognitively disoriented. The consulting physician prescribed a continuous administration of an antibiotic through a port in his upper chest.

Martin, in his delirious state, kept pulling out the IV. His family was called, as he required constant observation to prevent his pulling out of the needed IV. Neither of his daughters "had time" to watch over him, nor did the facility.

His therapist came to see him at the time of his session. His bed was stripped bare. "Where is Martin", she asked at the nurses' station.

"He passed. It was God's will", was the reply.

***Nita** came to an assisted living facility subsequent to the death of her beloved husband. One husband, five children. Only one daughter lived nearby.*

She had a severe case of cellulitis, but more than that, she just wanted to die. She missed her husband intensely and believed that only death could bring him close to her. That was all she wanted. That is what all she thought about. She was referred for psychotherapy for her depression.

Over time, Nita improved. She made some acquaintances with other residents. She surprised herself about how outgoing she had become. She liked to sit in the open places where people passed by, and she could say "hello". She got to the point where she could again sleep in the bed that she had shared with her husband and allowed herself some private time to speak to her husband's picture. Eventually, she could say to her therapist that she was "all right".

Then unfortunately, her cellulitis worsened to the point that she became septic and was hospitalized. A below-the-knee amputation of one of the legs was considered, but Nita rejected the idea.

The hospital suggested intensive care and treatment with antibiotics. The family said no to antibiotics, saying this would be an extraordinary measure. Nita was not consulted.

Why was the family able to decide this? Why did they decide for Nita that antibiotics represented extraordinary care?

Unlikely that Nita would have said that, but instead, Nita died.

Families must also be sensitive to the appropriateness of placement. When seniors complain, they may have good reasons.

Lillian who had had a mild left hemispheric stroke, recovered to the point that her language deficits were negligible, and physically she no longer showed impairment. Her son then moved her to an assisted living facility where she was bored and unhappy.

Prior to that, she had been at a facility associated with a rehabilitation center where she had been happy. The activities were stimulating. The people were friendly. She wanted to return there, especially as she was cognitively clear and mobile.

She made her wishes known to her son, but he, a teacher, was too busy. He ignored her every request and furthermore blocked her contact with the other facility, telling them she did not make any sense. He collaborated with the existing facility to make her stay there permanent. Lillian became extremely frustrated and depressed. She was then referred for psychotherapy. She reported to her therapist that she had called the previous facility herself, but that they refused to take her calls, because her son had told them that she could not be allowed back.

His motivation for blocking her wishes would always remain unknown. Lillian was not unreasonable, just unlucky. But then, by chance, luck intervened. Lillian's granddaughter came in from college to visit. She listened to Lillian and got things in motion. She chastised her father and facilitated the appropriate move for Lillian. A simple thing. A mistake turned around. But what if there had been no strong, sympathetic granddaughter.

Evelyn, a petite, proper 80 year-old-woman was placed in the same dementia unit of a facility where her now deceased sister-in-law had once been. She was quiet, sweet, and appealing, except for the incessant repetition of her particular delusion.

This was that she was going to be dead on December 25th. She would repeat that her husband had died on December 25th, that her mother and father had died on December 25th, and that her daughter had been shot to death in a mall on December 25th.

Logic had no effect on this delusion which she continued to share with everyone. December 25th came and went, she found herself alive, but still felt that perhaps next year.

There came a time, however, when she was diverted from her delusions by the upcoming marriage of her granddaughter. In her closet, hung a beautiful black-beaded dress, which she, as the grandmother, would wear as she walked down the aisle. When she started to mention December 25th, the staff easily diverted her attention to the upcoming spring wedding of her granddaughter.

Now there developed some complicated family interactions — leading to a decision that Evelyn was to be dis-invited from the wedding. A dilemma the family thought would be easily remedied, because Evelyn had a memory disorder. She was, after all, in the dementia unit!

The staff of the unit advised the family otherwise. All Evelyn could talk about was the wedding and wearing her beautiful black dress down the aisle. She fairly danced while describing and anticipating it.

For whatever reason, the family was entrenched in their decision.

The wedding came and went. The beautiful black and white event even made the newspapers. Evelyn had a vague idea that the wedding was due. The family had somewhat of a dilemma as the staff at the unit apprised them that they did not want to work with the fallout of Evelyn's discovery.

As a result, here is what the family did. They amassed twenty-five people- well known to Evelyn. They dressed her in her beautiful black dress and took her to the church where the wedding had occurred. They walked her down the aisle, smiling. They took pictures of her standing, sitting, smiling. They had a photographer superimposed her picture on a picture of the bride and groom.

Two framed picture, one of Evelyn walking down the aisle, and one with her with the bride and groom, were placed on her dresser

Evelyn would ponder out loud, "Did I go to that wedding?" Of course she did. There were the pictures on her dresser.

Was this a good family, or what?

Interventions by family have to be collaborative with the senior. Possible treatments must be discussed in advance and must consider life changes that may have to be made.

In a collaborative venture, what the senior would want must be known before the need becomes a reality. Asking the senior "what would you want if this happened, or in such and such a circumstance" is the beginning of working collaboratively.

Unfortunately, the increasingly dependent position of the senior can open the door for senior abuse in their emotional, financial, and living conditions. While most families are truly caring and helpful, this does not negate the alarming numbers of families and caregivers who, through ignorance or malevolence, are abusive to the elder parents.

Adult children who have taken advantage of their parents sometimes find themselves in a dilemma. Guilt makes them distance themselves from the senior. They rationalize and make excuses. This compounds the senior's emotional hurt. Instead of fleeing, it is always better to try to make up for misdeeds. Doing something good, apologizing, staying in their lives, spending time, taking them out, buying a small gift – even if it is from a thrift shop, begins the work of healing.

*So, **Ivan** was Pearl and Manny's son, unkind and suspicious, perhaps, even clinically pathological. His harsh manner towards the generous caring Pearl worsened after his father's death. How did the angels/devils conspire to make such a parent/child match?*

Anticipating a time when she would need help with her activities of daily living, Pearl approached her two children. She suggested adding each child's name to each of her two $30,000 certificates of deposit, in order to shelter her assets. She felt the money likely would soon be used to pay for needed care. "Of course", said the daughter. "I'll do it", said Ivan, "but you will never get the money back from me". Thinking the money would not be used for her care, anyway, Pearl conceded.

True to form, when Pearl needed care, Ivan gave nothing. After the money that the daughter had kept for her, was used up, Pearl was penniless.

Ivan was himself. Too busy to fly from the west coast to the east coast, but not too busy to send his family to live with Pearl for six months when he was out of work. Too busy to see Pearl for ten years, too busy to call or write – so no contact for the last three years of Pearl's life. Too busy to come to Pearl's funeral, which he insisted he would pay no part of. He explained and was adamant that all that was necessary was a plain pine box for Pearl's funeral.

A few years later, an unmarried uncle died and left an inheritance for his nieces and nephews. TWA quickly honored Ivan's request to immediately find him a seat on an east-bound plane so that he could make sure he got what due him.

So did he ever?

Professional Caregivers

While families are usually the primary caregivers for seniors, there has become an increasing need for professional caregivers.

The quality of these professional caregivers, in terms of attentiveness, competence, support, and reassurance are central to the senior's well-being. Professional caregivers include physicians, nurses, aides, therapeutic specialists, and administrators. All these individuals have a special interest in geriatrics. This is true at the higher end of caregivers. At the lower end of the caregiver continuum however, are aides and dining room and cleaning staff. These individuals are typically not paid well and have no special training or interest in the elderly.

Some people are simply not cut out to work with the senior population. They may find themselves working with seniors just because they need to make money to pay their bills. They apply for the job, whether or not it really attracts them. In the service of the seniors who need people who are aware of and sensitive to the transitions they are experiencing, these people should do something else

As people age, they become more dependent on others. In addition to the family, seniors also depend on professional caregivers. Their attention, responsiveness and reassurances are central to the senior's sense of well-being.

For seniors, whether at home or in assisted living, the caregivers now are physicians, nurses, aides, administrators and therapeutic specialists. Seniors increasingly rely on those in the helping professions. They expect them to provide their specialized skills, but they need more. They care, hope, time and understanding.

For the most part, professionals who work with seniors have a special interest and special training in geriatrics. Whether it is a physician, a therapist, a psychiatrist, etc., using a geriatric specialist optimizes the probability of getting more than just medical treatment.

Despite the special interest and training of professionals, seniors are heard to complain. For example, about physicians, "he didn't spend enough time, he didn't tell me anything". About nurses, "they don't answer the call bell, they don't understand". About dieticians and recreational directors, "they don't care, it makes no difference what we like".

As a result, there can be a difference between treatment and care.

Care

Care: noun, meaning concern, regard, diligence, nicety, thoughtfulness, serious attention of mind.

"Help me, help me." A visitor to a nursing home heard the call of a man in the place next to the person he was visiting. The man was curled up on a mat and could not turn himself. He was sore from being in one position. The visitor noticed that his call bell had not been answered in ten minutes.

Call it serendipity, call it fate. The next day, physicians and staff received a mailing from the nursing home. The Department of Health had recently completed a survey of the home and found the quality of care to be substandard. Too many bed sores and an inability to document that the schedules for turning and repositioning of patients was being adhered to.

Hope

Hope: Noun, meaning a wish, a desire; verb, meaning to look forward to, to feel confident.

Hope is that variable that helps us not give up. Perhaps, it is home that separates nursing home survivors from those who perish early on. Perhaps hope explains those unlikely stories of survival that we sometimes hear about. Hope comes from within, but also from those who are caregivers.

How disheartening to think that the professionals are too busy or too disconnected, or too "use to it", to be part of Hope.

How often does it seem that the death of a resident is expressed as a routine thing? "Oh, he passed yesterday". Maybe it is routine. Maybe it has to be. Maybe it would be too painful to repeatedly attach and lose. So professionals detach. Detach and hope cannot be partners.

The will to live is precious .. Patients want professionals to support their hope and desire to live.

> *The patient was a 74-year-old man in a nursing home. He suffered a left-hemisphere stroke which left him with extreme weakness of his right arm and leg, and with garbled speech. He had a type of expressive language disorder in which he knew what he wanted to say, but did not have the motor control to speak. He was aware and frustrated by his speech problem, and cried often. But he was lucky. He had a very supportive team, a wife who visited every day, encouraging children, and hard-working staff. The facility worked diligently with him on his walking. He could be seen in the hallways with a large, male physical therapist, holding him up by his belt, and helping him learn to walk. His wife brought him every puzzle and word game she could find. His speech*

*therapist worked to shape his mouth to re-learn how
to make words. The wife enlisted the aid of her son
and on weekends they would bring him home. They
took him home to show that home was where they
expected him to be. He worked hard. His crying spells
decreased. He began to walk better. His garbled speech
cleared to the point that he could be generally
understood. Everybody had hope that he would
improve, and one day, this man who had been so
impaired went home.*

Understanding

Seniors want to feel that caregivers will be sensitive to their
pains and worries. Staff have usually been around long enough so
that this understanding should come naturally.

*An 84-year-old wheelchair-bound, oxygen-
dependent resident lived in one part of a facility. His
wife lived in the Alzheimer's unit. He missed her and
unrealistically talked about bringing her to his room
to care for her. He visited her twice a day, making the
trip down long corridors to the other part of the
facility to see her. Gradually, through his own
observation, and through the counseling he received,
he began to understand what Alzheimer's meant.*

*One morning, the resident went to see his wife, but
could not rouse her. He called her name, shook her,
and got no response. He became wildly agitated,
calling out, "She's dead, she's dead". The nurse came
in and assured him that she was not dead, but was
taking sound naps during the day, because she was
not sleeping well at night.*

*The resident returned to his part of the facility. A
nurse at the nursing station repeated this episode to a*

colleague. She commented on his agitation, suggesting that, perhaps, he was becoming confused and demented, himself. She did not understand the distress and anxiety associated with the slow loss of a loved one to Alzheimer's. The resident's wife was actually not in the last stages of Alzheimer's. Nonetheless, he worried. The nurse reported that she thought that he was "losing it". However, he was right, because one week later, his wife died.

Time

Doctors and nurses, whether working through schedules or appointments, or on a shift, are rushed. The tension can be seen in their bodies. They will tell you they are overbooked and swamped with paperwork. Patients complain that their doctors rush in and out, that call bells are not answered, and that they don't get answers to their questions. Professionals acknowledge that they are rushed, feel pressured, frustrated, and sometimes, compromised in their ability to empathize.

A woman with a long history of psychiatric disorders moved to an assisted living facility. Her complaints focused on her anxiety. She was a rather attractive woman. She dressed in very bright clothing and used an abundance of make-up. She could not be missed. She attended activities, carved out a special work area for herself where she did her crafts, and was careful about complying with medical treatment and psychological recommendations. Despite this, her anxiety persisted. She was seen by a psychiatrist who consulted to the facility. He noted to her that she looked good, was active, and was doing fine. "No, no", she insisted, "but I feel awful, I get so upset". She was about to tell him about the physical symptoms that came with her anxiety, but he was gone. She complained, "He does not listen. He does not spend time. He did not change my medications."

Physicians complain that under managed care there is more pressure to see patients and less time to spend. They don't feel good about this. Physicians who go to a facility usually go there one day a week on a scheduled day in which a line of appointments await them. Some see this as pressure and not rewarding.

Nurses in facilities go home frustrated because they do not have time to do what they expected when they decided to become nurses. Yes, they acknowledge the call buzzers ring and ring. Sometimes, they become impervious to it. They become immune to the sound of patients calling out. They are told by the State that they must have enough staff for the patients, but this usually does not happen, especially in nursing homes where paperwork and documentation are a crucial part of licensing and inspections.

A nurse with forty years of experience stated that she did not know what she was getting into. Now she was immune to the sounds and the call bells, but was overwhelmed by the work. She thought she had to "stay the course" in the nursing home because that was all she knew and she needed the money and health insurance. "I feel that one day, I will be going from one side of the med cart to the other", she stated.

If an individual works with seniors and leaving is not possible because of financial needs, they must try to make the interactions with the seniors good natured. Taking a few moments to listen and share thoughts and ideas, rubbing their arm, bringing in something made from home, giving will make both feel better.

A suggestion for administrators, is to set up a system of evaluations by the residents for those providing hands-on services. Caregivers would be anonymously rated by the residents, and would get some kind of reward or bonus for the highest score of the week. This could serve two purposes – motivation for the staff and empowerment for the residents.

Chapter 3
FORMULATING A PLAN

Unless there is a sudden physical or cognitive change in a senior, ageing occurs gradually. As changes develop, a senior's ability to perform the activities of daily living (ADLs) are affected. This, then, is the time to consider alternative living situations and making a plan that "fits" the senior

Evaluating Changes

Assessment of the senior's ability to perform the basic ADLs (feeding oneself, maintaining good hygiene and dressing, and proper use of the bathroom), is the first step. Independent living also requires that the person be able to perform the more complex ADLs (shopping, cooking, following directions, taking medications correctly, communicating effectively, and managing one's finances). These are called Instrumental Activities of Daily Living.

Early signs of a decline in the ability to perform ADLs are the failure to prepare food and/or keeping spoiled food in the refrigerator, neglecting household duties (as evidenced by dirty pots and not keeping the house clean), neglect of personal hygiene (not bathing or brushing teeth, or wearing the same clothes day after day). Problems with short term memory may result in not taking medications or missing appointments. Driving a car can be dangerous if the senior gets lost, gets confused at exits, and drifts into the wrong lane. The need for safety will then dictate that the senior must give up driving privileges and find alternative means of transportation.

Signs of cognitive decline include failure to tend to financial matters, not opening mail, and not paying bills. Later cognitive changes can be manifested in inappropriate speech or behavior. A senior's awareness of these changes precipitates emotional reactions. It is not unusual then for them to become depressed, anxious, and apathetic.

When to Intervene

The best time to intervene is before there are signs of decline. Certainly, when a senior's health or safety are in jeopardy, it is time to intervene, but planning is best done before there is an urgent need for change.

Families who prepare early, explore options, and work together collaboratively make the senior's transition smoother. Emergency decisions, made without adequate research or input from the senior, have the poorest prognosis for the senior's adjustment.

Where planning is for a future or imminent change, the decisions should balance risk factors with the senior's comfort and independence.

Questions to consider when deciding whether to intervene are:

1. Can the senior's needs be met on a 24-hour-basis at home?

2. Is there adequate supervision for the senior who lives alone?

3. Can the family and caregivers provide adequately for the senior without them becoming emotionally and physically overstressed?

4. Have professionals recommended alternative living situations?

5. Does the senior's health require that they have consistent available medical monitoring?

6. Has the family's efforts to manage the senior's situation become less effective?

Preparing the Senior

It is common to avoid looking towards ageing for as long as possible. Minimizing the signs of decline unfortunately delays planning at a time when a senior will likely need help with their living situation. The sooner the planning, the better the prognosis for a good outcome.

Essential to a good outcome is planning with the senior. This means not just telling them about the plan or telling them things will have to change, but early on having active discussions, focusing on what the senior wants and envisions.

Sometimes it is easier to broach the topic indirectly. This may mean talking about another senior who needed to relocate, or referring to a TV program or magazine article that spoke to the issue. This can provide an opening to asking the senior about what alternatives they would consider if they needed care from others. Ask for their input. Timing is important. This means that the discussion is not so far in the future that it seems irrelevant and not so imminent that it is anxiety arousing.

Any change in life situation, be it moving to a facility, or having help in the home, can be disruptive and upsetting to the senior. It is important to realize that it is traumatic to move from a place that has been home for many years. The loss of familiar surroundings echoes earlier losses. Where the senior will spend the rest of their life is a major decision.

Seniors prefer to stay in their own homes. Some are fortunate and can. For others, health and safety issues determine that living at home is no longer an option. It is always easier for the senior if they are involved in the research, express their preferences, and feel others are mindful of their wishes. Seniors resist talking about change because they are fearful. They want to feel that they can still take care of themselves. Change implies that their abilities are declining. Seniors maintain "I can take care of myself. I'm not ready".

Planning is best if the family is not trying to force the senior into a decision. Therefore choose a time for discussion when everyone is relaxed and the setting is non-confrontational.

Listening

To understand what is important to a senior, you must listen. This means putting aside the caregiver's preferences, and listening to what the senior is expressing about their fears, concerns, and wishes.

Some families are better at giving advice, making suggestions, and placating than they are at listening. Listening means finding out what the senior wants, what realistically can be done, and then coming to terms with the facts.

Listening requires taking time and being mindful of where the senior is in terms of their needs and wishes. A senior's physical posture and eye contact will tell you about their comfort level. Giving feedback shows you have heard what the senior wants and that you are taking their point of view seriously. Families should not try to minimize or talk the senior out of their concerns. After listening, offer alternatives, if necessary, without pressure. Discuss possible solutions which best meet the senior's wishes. This helps avoid the seniors feeling ignored, cast aside, and abandoned.

Specifically, things to discuss with the senior are:

1. Their preferences about where they want to live. This should take into account their feelings about proximity to family, friends, and religious services.

2. Their financial resources. This affects what is actually available to them.

3. What kind of lifestyle and activities are pleasurable and fulfilling for them.

4. Legal issues, such as Power of Attorney, wills, advanced directives. Ask who they would want to handle things, if they were not able. Who would handle their money? Who would make legal decisions? Who would make medical decisions?

5. Do they have any particular wishes about their possessions; i.e., what they want to have with them and how they would distribute possessions.

There are times, though that despite a family's most diligent effort, the senior remains resistant and intransient. Sometimes old conflicts and disappointments are stirred up. Try to counter this by using the time to share memories and get closer. This can enhance your bond, rather than having an adversarial stance develop. This approach promotes gradual, but steady, progress in making a plan. If the senior has to move, assure them that their home will be well taken care of, and that they will get the much needed care at a facility.

Sometimes an outside resource such as a doctor or clergy may be enlisted. If the senior refuses to be part of the planning, the family must proceed anyway. Advise them that the best plan possible is being made so that they are not unprepared.

Sometimes, when the need for change is obvious, families are tempted to resolve things quickly. This gives a temporary feeling of relief. Be aware of the sales pitches and promotions promised by a facility that imply they can be all things to all people. It is tempting to believe their reassurances, but deciding without the senior's input is too often a prerequisite for failure.

All facilities have well-trained public relations staff who can reassure you that your relative will be happy and well-cared for. Facilities, however, vary widely – in their staffing patterns, their clientele, their amenities, their ambience, their setting (rural or urban), their proximity to the senior's former life, the physical plant, medical availability, mealtime arrangements, and so on. The optimal way to assure a "goodness of fit" is to accompany the senior on at least two visits to the facility.

Getting Organized

Crisis situations, on the other hand, require that the family come together to make a decision quickly. Crisis situations, as well as early planning, require that the family select one person to have primary responsibility. This person delegates responsibilities to others and is ultimately responsible to see the plan through. This person will develop a list of things with which the senior requires assistance. The list is divided into categories – things that family members can do, things the senior can do, and things that require outside intervention. In this collaborative planning, the needs, wishes, and ideas of all parties, especially the senior, are heard. The primary coordinator then works out the plan, makes the legal and financial arrangements, pays bills, if necessary, and keeps records of contacts with agencies and other providers or service.

The primary coordinator will also have to arrange for geriatric and competency assessments. Families should be prepared to seek guardianship if the senior resists or is incapable of making decisions. A Power of Attorney should be in place as early as possible.

If the family does not live near the senior, they will have to do long distance planning and organizing. If the senior lives alone, it is especially important to have proper knowledge of nearby resources. This means establishing a support system of friends and relatives. It is important to locate local agencies that can provide in-home services, such as Visiting Nurses, Meals on Wheels, and Senior Transit. It may be useful to engage the services of a geriatric care manager to oversee and visit the senior.

If planning without the assistance of a geriatric care manager, try to attend meetings with physicians and lawyers, and be there when assessments are made. Schedule medical visits when someone can go with the senior. This assures that accurate information about their condition and the services needed is obtained.

Part of planning requires that you become familiar with the senior's daily activities and schedules. Make a list of contact people for the senior. Include the names and numbers of professionals, agencies, family, and friends with whom the senior is involved. Sometimes, when seniors have to relocate, they lose contact with their friends, thus adding to feelings of loneliness.

Organize important documents in folders which include bank accounts, insurance policies, deeds, wills, names of relevant financial advisors and institutions, legal agencies, credit cards, Social Security benefits, other work-related benefits, income tax filings, valuables, assets, and debts. Sometimes it is helpful to engage the services of someone who specializes in geriatric law and estate planning.

Determining the necessary intervention or level or care can be complex. Sometimes it can be helpful to employ a Geriatric Care Manager. A Geriatric Care Manager is a professional who specializes in developing long term care plans for seniors. These professionals have a broad range of skills. They typically have a minimum of a bachelor's degree in nursing, social work, psychology, gerontology, or counseling. It is a good idea to select someone who is an accredited member of The National Association of Professional Geriatric Care Managers (telephone number 520-881-8008). Members in this association have had their credentials screened.

The Geriatric Care Manager is able to guide the family through assessments of the senior and is able to find local resources and facilities. They can also arrange for in-home health care and monitoring of the senior. They are particularly useful for families who do not live near the senior because they can provide crisis intervention when needed.

If the senior is to stay in their own home, a Geriatric Care Manager can assess the home for safety and make recommendations. They are able to assess the senior's ability to perform the Activities of Daily Living and the Instrumental Activities of Daily Living. Their evaluation includes a description of the senior's strengths and limitations as well as their social, emotional, and physical state.

Geriatric Care Managers also provide information about where to obtain legal, medical, and financial assistance. They are familiar with agencies that can offer services in the home.

In choosing a Geriatric Care Manager it is important to find one who has not only observed and visited local resources, but who evaluates them on an ongoing basis. They also should have clinical understanding of the family dynamics and the emotional needs of the senior. The latter is important because conflicts may occur in the family with the senior and the care manager must be able to intervene therapeutically.

After completing an assessment, the geriatric care manager brings the family and the senior together to review options. Once an option is chosen the care manager can assist in implementing it and may provide support to the senior. They also do follow up visits to assess the senior's adjustment to the plan.

Whether the plan is monitored by the family or a geriatric care manager, it is necessary to insure that the senior is adjusting socially and emotionally, that all services necessary are being coordinated, and that the required standard of care is maintained for the senior.

Assessment: The comprehensive assessment is the first step in making a plan. The goal of the assessment is to find the least restrictive setting for the senior. The assessment will determine the level of care that is needed. Levels of care range from light supervision (such as help with cleaning and meals) to moderate care (which involves daytime assistance with ADLs), to 24-hour care either in a facility or in the senior's home.

Levels of care vary from "least restrictive" which is independent living with mild intervention, to Alzheimer's Units or nursing homes, for those seniors who are totally unable to care for themselves. When making a decision about a level of care the family should try to look ahead and anticipate how the senior's need for care may change. Questions to consider when choosing a facility are: Can the facility move the senior to more intensive level of care if needed? Can the families bring someone in to the facility to care for their relative if that is needed? If the choice is for the senior to remain at home with support services, does the family have a plan in place if more intensive care, such as medical or nursing care becomes necessary?

The Goodness of Fit: Deciding on whether a senior will remain in their home with support or move to a facility is not easy. If reality dictates that the senior must move, the move should be presented as beneficial, emphasizing that it can be positive as well as necessary.

Factors which must be taken into account when deciding between home care and a facility.

1. Is the senior a social or private person? Do they like being around others or would they be uncomfortable if they had to eat with others or share a room?

2. How central to their identity is their independence and ability to have choices? Would they feel constrained by

the schedules of a facility – i.e. the predetermined meals and activities?

3. Can they occupy themselves or would they be lonely in their homes if they had restricted mobility?

4. Would they be able to relax and enjoy having their activities scheduled and planned by others?

5. Can they adjust and change or have they always been set in their ways?

If the decision is made that the senior will remain in their home, the caregiver must ask questions of themselves. How much time, energy and scheduling can they do? What are the caregiver's emotional resources? Do they have their own support system? Are their expectations about being a caregiver realistic or will they be at risk for burn out?

Before deciding to move a senior to a particular facility, it is important to observe the residents, the staff, and the program. Ways to assess different facilities will be described in a later chapter. Some things to explore though are: Who is in charge- of administration, maintenance, therapies, dietary service, medical decision, housekeeping, and activities? Learn who will have direct contact with your senior – which particular aides and caregivers will be assigned to the senior and who is the person to contact if concerns arise. Find out how receptive the staff are to keeping an open dialogue. How available are they to giving and receiving updated information about the senior? If the facility has care meetings, are families encouraged to attend them? These meetings are regularly scheduled reviews of the treatment plans. This is when goals and progress are evaluated and revised.

If concerns arise which cannot be resolved with the facility, is there an available Ombudsman? (An Ombudsman is an independent person from the community who helps resolve problems between the resident, family, and the facility).

The telephone number of the Ombudsman should be posted in a visible place.

Some considerations to be made in selecting a facility are:

1. Is the senior more comfortable in a city or rural setting?

2. If they do not live near family would they rather go to a facility close to where they lived or relocate to be near family?

3. How accessible are they to the outside world? Can they walk or get transportation to shopping, religious services, and their physicians? Will they be comfortable having to depend on the facility or the family to get out?

4. Is there homogeneity in background and interest with other residents? If the senior is relocating to be near family, will they feel isolated and estranged in the new area where they do not know anyone?

5. What kinds of activities are offered? Is there enough stimulation for the senior? Are the activities provided those that they would like and go to?

6. What is the level of formality in the facility? Is the senior more comfortable in a casual or formal setting?

7. Will they have their own room or share a room? Sometimes finances determine this. For some seniors privacy is very important and they would sacrifice the amenities of a more expensive facility for the sake of privacy. Other seniors do not like being alone and would welcome an arrangement where they would have a roommate.

8. What is the availability and accessibility of friends and family for visits?

9. What is the physical set up of the facility? Is it on one level? Do residents have to use an elevator? Some are

uncomfortable with this. Are there long hallways from their rooms to the dining room or to activity rooms?

Many factors go into making a choice – finances, practicalities, availability of facilities, and most importantly the comfort of the senior. The goal is to make a plan that will work over the long haul.

The Geriatric Assessment

The geriatric assessment is often the first step in making a plan for a senior. It is a comprehensive medical, psychological, and social assessment. The information gathered covers the physical and psychosocial status of the senior and their needs, resources, strengths, and weaknesses.

Evaluations usually take place in a medical center that has a multi-disciplinary team which specializes in geriatrics. Part of the evaluation should also take place in the senior's home. The latter allows for observation of how the senior functions at home as well as assessing the physical set-up of the home. Members of the multi-disciplinary team typically include an internist, a social worker, a neurologist, a nurse, an occupational therapist, a psychiatrist, and a psychologist.

The evaluation may require several days. It will probably include laboratory tests and perhaps imaging studies, such as a CAT scan or an MRI. At the end of the evaluation, the team meets to formulate a diagnosis and make a treatment plan. The goal of the evaluation is to come up with a plan that will allow the senior to live as independently as possible. The team then meets with the family and senior to discuss both the results of the assessment and the treatment plan. Written summaries are given to the family and to the family physician.

Components of the Geriatric Assessment: Central to the evaluation is a total assessment of the senior's health status. This includes current physical problems, previous medical history, the family medical history, medications (dosages and history of medications), hearing and vision screening, assessment of mobility, gait, continence, diet, and nutrition.

It is essential to have accurate knowledge of the senior's physical condition (including illnesses and disabilities), in order to plan correctly. Information should be obtained from a senior's family, caregivers, and physicians, in order to get the most complete medical picture. Several illnesses present with the same symptoms, and some serious illnesses present with psychological symptoms first. Therefore it is important to determine whether the symptoms have a physical or psychological basis.

Knowing the family history (or parents and siblings), their illnesses, age of death, and cause of death can be predictive of what a senior may expect.

The senior's medication history and regime are an important part of the physical assessment. Medications can have psychological and physical side effects. Elderly individuals typically take many medications. Sometimes they have been on the same dosage for years, even though their metabolism has changed. The effects of being on the same dosage may be intensified or even toxic. Some of their medication may interact with others and lessen their effectiveness or have a negative effect. All medication should be listed, including over the counter drugs, herbs, vitamins, and health foods. Some medications such as antibiotics and psychotropic drugs can interact and affect the central nervous system. Seniors sometimes take old, obsolete prescriptions or they may not take their medications which were prescribed for them. Some of their medications may have negative effects if the senior is combining them with alcohol or other substances.

In addition to the above, seniors should always be asked about their use of alcohol and tobacco, their appetite, and sleep functions, as well as bowel and bladder functions.

The Psychological Evaluation: A major part of the assessment is the cognitive and emotional evaluation. In terms of cognitive functions, expressive and receptive language, short and long term memory, and immediate recall should be tested. Visual-spatial ability and abstract reasoning should also be determined as they factor in to an individual's ability to live independently. The information gathered will allow for a differential diagnosis between cognitive and psychological conditions. This is important because some illnesses such as depression and dementia present with similar symptoms. For example, both can present with symptoms of confusion, cognitive slowing, difficulty concentrating, and impaired problem solving ability. A differential diagnosis is central to formulating treatment interventions.

A major part of the psychological evaluation is the assessment of current and past psychiatric disorders. Depression and anxiety found in the elderly population are often associated with their life changes. The decline in their physical state, life changes (including the loss of family and friends), and the need to relocate can exacerbate the condition.

An often under-diagnosed and unrecognized problem in the elderly is substance abuse, especially alcohol abuse. Seniors may use alcohol to self-medicate for depression and anxiety. Many of these seniors do not have a history of abusing alcohol or drugs, but begin using substances following a loss or major change in their life. Alcohol abuse in seniors may not be identified if they live alone, or if there is no close contact with family or caregivers. It should be noted that a senior's tolerance for alcohol, and likewise, for prescription and over-the-counter medications, is lower because of their metabolic changes.

Risk factors which precipitate alcohol abuse in seniors include loss (not only of people through death or distance) but also of their physical abilities, mobility, their homes and their jobs. Genetic factors, co-morbid psychiatric disorders, gender (males are more likely to abuse alcohol), early abuse in life, loneliness, boredom, and self-esteem issues, are also risk factors for alcohol abuse.

Seniors can also abuse over-the-counter and prescription medication. Often they have had the same prescription for long periods of time. Some of these drugs have a psychologically addicting quality. Risk factors for drug and medication abuse also include chronic pain and sleep disturbance.

Activities of Daily Living (ADLs): The geriatric assessment evaluates the ability to perform the Activities of Daily Living. Again these include, bathing, grooming, eating regular meals, and toileting. The senior's ability to transfer from a bed to a chair unassisted, and to sit down and stand up unassisted are also part of basic ADLs.

Instrumental Activities of Daily Living (IADLs) are also assessed. These are more complex functions such as meal preparation, shopping, cooking, and medication. Other IADLs are the ability to clean the house, use public transportation, manage ones finances, use the telephone, seek help when needed, and follow medical advice. Because these are more complex that the basic ADLs, these are areas where impairment often shows up earlier.

The Safety of the Living Situation: Perhaps the primary factor for requiring seniors to transition is safety. The safety of their premises and of their neighborhood has major implications for the living arrangement they will have. Frequently it is repeated falls that bring a senior to a facility. Therefore the home should be evaluated for safety hazards, as should be the safety of the neighborhood. The senior who goes into the neighborhood alone should be able to get places by themselves safely.

Social Support System: Friends, family and caregivers comprise the social support network of the senior. The primary caregiver should be evaluated in terms of the ability to cope with the stress of being a caregiver, and their availability to the senior when necessary. If the caregiver is overwhelmed, they may become at risk, physically and emotionally. The social support system also has a formal component which includes physicians, social agencies, and programs which are available to the senior.

Socialization and Activities: Part of the assessment should evaluate the senior's quality of life. Information should be gathered about the availability of social interactions with others and whether the senior leaves the house or if they are isolated.

Involvement in leisure activities such as walking, reading, watching TV, listening to music, exercising, and participating in religious activities are also part of assessing the quality of the senior's living arrangement.

Chapter 4
FINANCIAL CONSIDERATIONS

As previously noted, finances for seniors are complicated. This speaks to the need for a good financial planner whose goal is to work for what is best for their client. The financial planner should be certified by the Board of Standards as a "Certified Financial Planner". That person should work with the senior's lawyer and accountant to make sure all investments, wills, trusts, and living arrangements are in place.

Nowadays, seniors do not typically dream about "the golden days". Rather they often have to budget carefully and cut back on their expenses. Social Security does not nearly cover the current cost of living. And while it has long been assumed that it will be there, younger generations are forewarned that Social Security funds may be exhausted before their generation reaches the age at which they can collect.

Money is a potential source of anxiety for seniors.

- Seniors are afraid that they will run out of money and will not have enough money to last them the rest of their lives.

- Seniors are afraid that they will be a financial burden on their families.

- Seniors are afraid of being taken advantage of financially.

- Seniors get anxious when they don't know what is happening with their money.

- Seniors are afraid that if they become ill there won't be enough money for their care.

It is therefore important for seniors to know what their assets are and how best to manage them.

Some seniors find it sensitive and embarrassing to have to depend on others for the management of their finances. This is especially true if they have to ask for their money from adult children or from staff at a facility. It is also hard for them to worry that their money is not being spent the way they want.

Even if seniors voluntarily gave up the management of their money, the feelings of independence and control are compromised. Families can inadvertently increase this discomfort by avoiding talking with the senior about finances. Families, therefore, must be aware that just as they had to find the time to talk about living arrangements, so they must also find opportunities to talk about money.

Financial abuse of a senior can result in alienation within the family. The senior is hurt and angry – the wrongdoer feels guilty and embarrassed.

> *After the death of his wife, **Fred**, a 76-year-old man, with a history of diabetes and coronary artery disease, moved to an assisted living facility. His eldest daughter had Power of Attorney. She managed his Social Security, pension, and VA benefits. Despite his having adequate financial resources, his daughter convinced him that he was only able to afford a semi-private room.*
>
> *Fred and his roommate were not compatible. The roommate watched television into the late hours, and what was most unnerving, frequently "missed" in the bathroom. Fred could not understand why he could not have his own room. He had many sources of income. What he did not know that, over the course of many months, his daughter had not been paying the bill.*
>
> *The administrator of the facility questioned Fred's daughter who explained that she had a "problem" son who needed the money. She used her father's benefits*

for her son's needs. Fortunately, the facility and Fred's other daughter intervened. Power of Attorney was given to the more responsible daughter. Fred's funds were appropriately directed to his care. He was able to get a room for himself, his mood improved, his physical complaints decreased, and he became involved in the activities of the facility.

When becoming involved in the senior's finances, the best approach is the direct one. Seniors should know that there is a need for them to say how they want to live and be taken care of should the need arise. Questions to resolve include, how do they want their money to be managed? What reserves do they have for emergencies and funeral expenses? Senior may be reluctant to reveal their assets, but they should at least provide a list of their accounts, investments, insurance policies, deeds, safety deposit boxes, and other important papers.

If money is not the root of all evil, it certainly can create conflict and divisiveness in families, especially when decisions must be made about finances and inheritances. Whether the amount of assets is significant or not, money stirs up old hurts, conflicts, and jealousies. A parent's possessions, whether it be a pair of earrings or thousands of dollars, can be the source of intense conflict. It is, therefore, important to have discussions about possessions when the senior is alive and able to articulate their wishes. Tackling this sensitive subject can prevent their heirs fighting over items of inheritance after the senior's death. In deciding how things will be distributed, it is advisable that the family get together to specify whether there is something that is especially meaningful or appealing to one of them. It is helpful for the senior to have input from the heirs when deciding how their possessions will be dispersed.

It is helpful to have a list of possessions and valuables that can be made available and for family members to indicate their preferences. For some families, this is just too awkward or potentially conflictual. It is therefore helpful to hire a financial planner.

A financial planner can also help the senior budget their money and manage their assets. The senior should be the one who decides whether it is a family member or independent planner who will budget and manage their money. Any person who manages the senior's finances should keep a record of bills and payments, and review them regularly with the senior. This is reassuring to the senior and enhances their feeling of control. Considering how important it is to the senior, it is surprising how infrequently this happens. Whether the senior is living in their own home, or living in a facility, they need to feel informed and confident about their financial situation.

After a senior has moved to a facility, they will still want to know what is happening to their house and belongings. Decisions about the maintenance and services for the house should be discussed with a senior.

An astounding number of seniors who move to a facility are never told when their house is sold, what the proceeds were, and most alarming for them, what became of their valued possessions. "Don't sell my things" is their silent cry.

Estate Planning

All seniors should do estate planning. Many seniors underestimate the value of their estate because they do not include their home, cars, household items, and other belongings as part of the estate.

It is important to do estate planning with a lawyer who specializes in this. It is also important to draw up a will and appoint an executor of the estate. There also should be someone who is designated to be the Durable Power of Attorney.

Seniors who wish to lower their taxable estate can transfer assets to others while they are alive. Under the Annual Gift Tax Exclusion, in 2015, individuals are allowed to give up to $14,000 per year to an unlimited number of people without incurring Federal gift tax. Seniors should also be careful in "gifting" money in order to shelter it. Sometimes, a "gift" remains a gift, if the "giftee" gets greedy or irresponsible with the money.

Efforts to shelter real estate from individual taxes are a special consideration. There are pros and cons to making children or grandchildren co-owners of real estate in order to shelter inheritance. A potential problem is that if the transfer is deemed improper, it can jeopardize eligibility for Medicaid. The senior's residence, though, can be placed in a trust for children or grandchildren, who would own the residence in name and be the landlord to the senior. A grandchild, for example, might pay minimal taxes on the rental and the home can be passed down to the heirs for their use.

Trusts

Establishing a trust is a means of setting aside monies in order to reduce estate taxes. In establishing a trust, assets are transferred to a trustee who manages the assets for beneficiaries, or manages assets while the senior is still alive. A stipulation can be made as to how monies in the trust are dispersed. This is useful if the senior has concerns about the misuse or wasting of their money. Trusts allow the person designated as Power of Attorney to carry out the senior's financial wishes after they are deceased.

Financial Budgeting

It is crucial for seniors to do their post-retirement financial planning early. This means making a realistic post-retirement budget, not spending more than one can afford in the pre-retirement years, and not letting credit card debt accumulate. The current post-retirement period is significantly longer than it was for previous generations. It will require relatively more funds than parents and grandparents had saved. Social Security alone will NOT cover expenses. Maintaining one's lifestyle may be a challenge and seniors may experience sticker shock when it comes to maintaining the lifestyle they were used to.

Seniors should plan to live longer. Ninety years of age is not uncommon and even living to be 100 will not be a rarity in the future. Many seniors will live 25-30 years after retirement. Seniors have been heard to express that they worry that their money will run out before they die.

A recent online article (www.fox.business.com. 03/07/2011) reported that the Society of Actuaries found that the baby boomers generation is actually inadequately planning for retirement. To more accurately see what retirement will cost you, go online to www.moneyforlifeguideonline.com.

Medical Costs

Medicare is a health program funded by the government. Initially, it was designed for people over 65 and for disabled individuals under age 65. Medicare has two parts, A and B. The cost of **Medicare Part A** is taken directly out of one's Social Security check. Medicare Part A covers inpatient hospital care and is available to anyone who is eligible for Social Security benefits. Medicare also pays for the first 60 days of inpatient hospitalization, minus the first day, which is deductible. From day 61-150, the co-insurance increases. There is no Medicare coverage after the first 150 days, and there is a Limited Lifetime benefit for inpatient psychiatric hospitalization.

Medicare also pays for skilled nursing care in a nursing home or rehabilitation facility after the senior has been released from a hospital. The first 20 days are fully paid by Medicare. Thereafter, days 21-100 have a coinsurance payment. Medicare also pays for health care services delivered to the home. These include physical therapy, speech therapy, intermittent skilled nursing, home health aides, hospice care, and medical equipment. It does not pay for personal care, such as help with ADLs, if that is the only care needed.

Medical costs not covered by Medicare Part A are either paid out-of-pocket, or by **Medicare Part B**. Medicare Part B pays for 80% of outpatient services, such as doctors, laboratory tests, health screenings, emergency care, diabetes self-management, vaccines, and 50% of mental health costs. Not all providers accept the amount of payment assigned by Medicare Part B. In some states, physicians charge more than the Medicare allowable rate and bill the patient for the balance.

The premiums for Medicare Part B can be high for seniors. As with any insurance, seniors should do comparative shopping. Generally, the better the benefits, the higher the premium. Medicare Part B also pays for medical equipment and outpatient therapies, if prescribed by a physician. There is no limit on the services, but the patient must be evaluated every 30 days by the prescribing physician. Medicare does not pay for home care for chronic conditions. It also has limitations on the amount of skilled care received in the home. Among the things not covered by Medicare Part B are prescription drugs, hearing aids, dental care, and private duty nursing.

Medicare Part B premiums and deductibles are always rising to the point where they impact on Social Security costs-of-living adjustments to those who collect Social Security benefits.

Not all facilities are Medicare and Medicaid approved. A facility must be inspected and meet Federal standards. Some facilities set aside a certain number of beds for Medicare and Medicaid patients. If a senior is in one of these facilities, and their private resources run out they cannot be forced to leave. Facilities which do not have Medicare or Medicaid provisions, may make a senior leave when they have used up their private resources.

Because Medicare has limitations, some seniors obtain supplemental insurance from Private Medicare Plus plans. These have additional benefits, such as prescription drugs. Some are similar to HMO plans in that the senior is restricted to using certain hospitals and doctors and must get a referral to see a specialist. Medicare Managed Care plans have varying benefits and costs. The Medicare internet site (www.medicare.gov) and a toll free number 1-800-MEDICARE can provide information and booklets which can assist in comparing prices for policies.

Medigap policies provide coverage for things that Medicare does not pay for. There is a monthly premium and the senior can select the doctor or hospital of their choice. They also do not need a referral to see a specialist. The premium and benefits vary from company to company. In comparing policies, the senior must consider if they need to see a particular doctor, and what it will cost if they go out of network for care. Policies should be compared in terms of inpatient benefits, mental health benefits, substance abuse benefits, provision for specialists, routine screenings, dental and visual services, outpatient rehabilitation, laboratory and diagnostic tests, radiation therapy, emergency care, and transportation to medical appointments.

Some states have prescription programs for seniors who meet specific income requirements. Usually, the plan has a deductible, which once met, offers generic or brand-name medications at set reduced amounts with co-pays. Some of these plans have helpful features, such as reminding a senior when a prescription needs to be refilled, delivering medications to the enrollee, or mailing prescriptions, if the enrollee is away from home. Some plans have no membership fees and others offer substantial savings over pharmacy prices.

There are also programs for seniors who do not have the financial resources to pay for medications. One such program is the Free Medication Foundation (1-573-966-3333, internet site www.Freemedicationfoundation.com). This program only requires a processing fee for each prescription.

Medical Assistance provides medication for qualifying individuals with limited incomes. There is a deductible which must be met before medications can be obtained. Information on prescription drug assistance programs can be obtained by calling 1-800-MEDICARE or online. www.medicare.gov. Select "Prescription Assistance Programs". There are also Medigap plans sold by insurance companies which have varying benefits.

In selecting Medicare, or Medigap plans, it is important to try to anticipate what benefits a senior will need and what the out-of-pocket costs will be.

Costs for seniors always go up. In 2010, it was reported that the average for a private room in a nursing home had risen 4.6% in one year - that is an average cost of $83,655. The average charge for assisted living rose by 5.2% in one year to an average fee of $3,293 a month.

There are also insurance plans (**Medicare Part D**) that pay for prescription drugs. Prescription drugs continue to be one of the biggest expenses for seniors. Again the better the coverage for medications, the more expensive is the plan. Typically a plan will have a significantly lower copay for generic, than for the brand-named drugs. All prescription drug plans have a so-called, "doughnut hole". The doughnut hole is somewhat a difficult concept. The doughnut hole represents a combination of monies paid by the insurer and the insured for medication. Once this combined amount paid is reached the dreaded "doughnut hole" kicks in and the rules of payment change. The insured senior pays just about all of their brand medication costs. Generic brands are covered and generally cost much less than expensive brand names. If brand-name medications are necessary, the senior pays the entire costs when they are in the "doughnut hole" and this can be very costly. Once a certain amount of out-of- pocket monies have been paid, all medication costs are covered.

MEDICAID

Medicaid has strict provisions and restrictions to prohibit the transferring of assets in order to qualify for benefits. There are penalties and periods of ineligibility, and disqualification of benefits incurred for assets distributed in order to "spend down".

The transfer of assets, for the three-year period prior to application of benefits, must be accounted for, with proof that it was not given in order to qualify for Medicaid. Medicaid presumes that assets distributed were made in order to obtain benefits and, therefore, calculates a disqualification period during which benefits cannot be obtained. This is based on the amount Medicaid was paying and the value of the assets transferred.

There are monthly limits on income and limits on assets that are used to determine eligibility for Medicaid. Seniors should check with Medicaid for eligibility requirements.

One of the benefits of Medicaid is that, once the requirements to receive it have been met, it does pay for long-term nursing home care. Individuals with long-term chronic illnesses, such as Parkinson's disease or Alzheimer's disease, will then be able to receive custodial care in a nursing home. Medicare does not pay for such care.

Medicaid will pay for the difference between the amount a senior receives for Social Security and the cost of the care in the facility.

In determining eligibility for Medicaid, resources that are counted include cash, savings, investments, IRA's, non-residential real estate, recreational vehicles, and having more than one vehicle. Resources that are not included are a residence (if a spouse or if the senior intends to return to it), a car, household goods, personal items, burial needs, and an IRA (for the spouse not receiving Medicaid).

Long-Term Care Insurance

This type of insurance is purchased to cover costs in the event custodial care is needed. It is obtained to guarantee that payment will be made for services in a facility, in the community, or in the home.

Companies that market this type of insurance, claim that it allows families and seniors to keep their assets. The down side of this insurance is that it can be very costly. Benefits vary considerably from policy to policy. The premiums paid though are eligible for a tax deduction, and discounts are available if the spouse also purchases long term care insurance.

As policies vary, it is important to look at several plans and types of coverages. Generally the earlier one enrolls in a plan, the lower the monthly premium. This must be weighed against the longer time of paying premiums.

It is advisable to consider long term care insurance when the senior is still capable of performing the Activities of Daily Living. Once a senior has an illness, it is more difficult and more expensive to get insurance. Companies may also deny benefits if they find there was an undisclosed, pre-existing condition when the policy was obtained.

It is also somewhat of a guessing game to anticipate at what point in the senior's life long-term care insurance will be needed. Approximately 50% of people over 85 require long-term care and more than six per cent of 65 plus seniors living in nursing homes also do.

Selecting a policy can be complicated, as the costs and options vary depending on the policy selected. Logically, the higher the amount of coverage the higher the premium. The length of the policy, whether it be for a specified period of years or unlimited, also effects the monthly premium.

Long-term care insurance policies have a deductible, called an elimination period. This is the time before payment begins. The shorter the elimination period, the more expensive the policy. Also for consideration are various supplemental benefits such as inflation protection and waiver of premiums, which occurs if the policy holder is ill and unable to pay the premium. Having an inflation protector rider built into the policy is important if one obtains a policy early.

The average period of time a senior will need care is three to five years. If one wants the security of coverage for chronic or long-term illness, a longer policy should be selected.

There are formulas and considerations that help determine whether it is advisable to buy long-term care insurance. A senior with limited assets, who has trouble paying for their basic needs, and relies on Social Security, is not a candidate for long-term care insurance. A senior with considerable income and assets may want to protect their assets, and will likely be able to pay the premiums. A rule of thumb is: if the cost of the policy will be 5% or less of the anticipated retirement income, it should be considered. If it will cost more than 5% it is not recommended. The benefits paid by long-term care insurance are usually not included in taxable income.

Services that are covered by long-term care insurance include skilled care, nursing home care, assisted living facilities, adult day care centers, personal and home health care, and services in certain community facilities. Some policies have restrictions on who can provide care, while others are less restrictive. Benefits are typically not paid for mental diseases, addictions, suicide attempts, illness resulting from war, or treatment that the government has paid for.

Eligibility to begin to receive benefits is determined by what are called benefit "triggers." These vary from policy to policy. Before these "trigger points" are met certain expenses must be paid by the individual. Usually the "trigger" is the individual's inability to perform three out of six, or two out of five of the Activities of Daily Living. Another "trigger" is cognitive impairment which necessitates the need for constant supervision.

Aside from costs, what the policy covers is the most important consideration on deciding on long-term care insurance. These considerations are the type of facility covered, the assurance that the policy cannot be cancelled as long as the premiums are paid on time, and the daily benefit paid by the policy. Inflation protection is a feature which protects against having to pay higher premiums because of an increased in cost of care. There are also non-forfeiture benefits which continue the policy if the policy holder cannot pay the premium. Some policies have a limit on the total benefit in terms of years or dollars. Longer benefit periods or larger amounts pain out, cost more.

When purchasing a policy it is important to select a stable company, because it is likely that the policy will be purchased years before it is needed. The history and rating of the company should be checked with Standard and Poors. Also check Moody's investors' service (212-553-0337) and a Shopper's Guide to Long Term Care Insurance for the National Association of Insurance Commissioners (1-816-783-8300). On the internet check A.M. Best Company, www.ambest.com.

Long-term care insurance may be affordable and provide security for some, but can be expensive and risky. There is potential for the loss of all monies that were paid in, and there can be restrictions on receiving benefits. There may also be the possibility that the company will not be in existence when the benefits are needed. Consumer Reports advised waiting until age 65 to obtain coverage.

Reverse Mortgages

Reverse Mortgages allows seniors to borrow against the equity they have in their home. Up front costs are minimal and the fees can even be wrapped into the loan. The money withdrawn can be used to pay off the remaining mortgage, can be drawn out in a lump sum, in a monthly check, or as needed. The amount borrowed does not have to be repaid until the house is sold and the amount repaid can never be greater than the amount the house sells for. The cash that is available from a reverse mortgage depends on the value of the house.

In contrast to a typical mortgage where there is falling debt and rising equity over time, the reverse mortgage is a system of rising debt and falling equity over time. Reverse mortgages can have a large impact on your estate. If the equity in the house is used for the senior's expenses, there will be less left for inheritance by heirs.

In taking out a reverse mortgage, seniors should be careful that they do not increase their assets and jeopardize their getting their other benefits, such as Social Security which has a limit on assets. It is therefore important to limit the amount taken to what one expects to spend in a given month.

It is possible that with a reverse mortgage there will come a time when there is no equity left in the house. If this happens the senior can still stay in their house without making monthly payments and this can be appealing. Another benefit is that the money received is not taxable. There are no income requirements to obtaining a reverse mortgage. The senior only has the responsibility in keeping the home in good condition and continuing to pay the taxes on it.

A reverse mortgage must be the first and only mortgage on the home. This means that if money is owed from a previous mortgage it must be paid off first, possibly by using some of the money from the reverse mortgage.

The debt owed on a reverse mortgage is the amount taken plus interest and advances. If when the home is sold, it is worth more than the debt owed, the senior or the estate keeps the balance.

There are three types of reverse mortgages. 1. The Single Purpose – which specifies how the money can be used. 2. A Federally Insured Mortgage – which can be used for any purpose. These have somewhat higher fees than a Single Purpose reverse mortgage. 3. The Proprietary Mortgage, which is obtained on expensive homes which provide a larger loan advance. These are the most costly reverse mortgages.

Deciding if whether a reverse mortgage is right for a senior is complicated. Here again it is wise to consult the financial planner to decide if this commodity is advisable and if so which one to select.

Chapter 5
LEGAL CONSIDERATIONS

Legal issues for seniors present novel and unique challenges. They are important legal matters that must be tended to that under different circumstances might be left aside. For seniors, however, not tending to their unique legal affairs can result in their wishes being disregarded or even abused. The absence of what many think is obvious (i.e., a will, or an advanced directive), can open the door to conflict and manipulation, and even mercenary acts by caregivers, families, vendors, and institutions.

It is always best that legal matters, such as wills, finances, and advanced directives, be set up early. Decisions about these issues should be written down and filed legally while the senior is competent and able to specify how they want legal matters handled. Preferably, the above means engaging the services of a lawyer who specializes in geriatric law. A senior who uses a lawyer makes it less stressful and conflictual for the family. This planning should also specify how decisions are made if the point comes when the senior is no longer mentally competent. Thus an advocate needs to be appointed (a person with power-of-attorney, durable power-of-attorney, or guardian). Careful consideration must be given to who will be the advocate, not only in name, but in actuality.

Families who become involved in making medical decisions should honor the HIPAA laws and not try to get around them. HIPAA laws were written to protect an individual's privacy with regard to their medical condition. Nowadays, prior to a medical appointment, patients sign a contract which ensures that their medical information will not be released without their consent. This also protects them from others being involved with or party to their treatment, if they do not agree.

HIPPA laws, however, have been known to be abused by persons with power of attorney in terms of both invasiveness and decisions about treatment.

All too frequently medical decisions are made without a senior's being consulted, or because the senior is in a facility without access to an impartial advocate. It is alarming to note how families can get around HIPAA regulations and how agencies and facilities can knowingly or unknowingly collude with this.

A 56-year-old woman in an assisted living facility was facing her second bout with breast cancer. She recently had lost her husband and a son to cancer and was paralyzed as to what course of treatment to follow. Time was passing and the recommendation was made that she be seen by a psychologist. This helped her to move forward and make choices. The family, though, was upset that the therapist had questioned the resident's choice of a hospital. They then said that they did not understand the resident's grief issues or her continued need for counseling. They were abrupt, would not discuss the mother's needs, and stated that the psychological services should be stopped. This was not the resident's wish but she feared angering and isolating her family.

Power of Attorney (POA)

To give someone Power of Attorney is to potentially grant them major influence over one's life. The giver and the receiver of Power of Attorney must be sensitive. POWER - the one who accepts it is expanded, the one who gives it is diminished. If you are a senior living in your own home, or living in a facility, you are signing a legal document which allows someone else to handle your personal affairs under certain circumstances. These circumstances are either you are unable to make your own decisions, or you do not wish to make your own decisions.

Power of Attorney is actually necessary when an individual has lost the ability to make good decisions due to cognitive impairment. However instances occur when the senior is still competent to make decisions, but is kept out-of-the loop.

It is, therefore, important that the POA be set up in such a way that seniors still have access to the status of their finances, assets, legal, and medical documents. There should also be a provision that assures seniors' recourse when such access is not given them.

Even if seniors have not given someone a POA, their rights may be violated by a family member or caregiver. This is an extremely risky situation for the senior who has put a family member's name on a bank or financial account, or who had someone else with access to their belongings and assets.

Howard, a rather emotionally labile man, lived in an assisted living facility in southern New Jersey.

His son had a lifetime history of borrowing and misspending his father's money. He had further engaged in many illicit financial transactions. He was quite slick and reputed to be a skilled cheat and operator. He had managed to sell his father's condo, pocketed the profits, promised to give them to his father, but instead, kept depleting his father's funds. He finally placed his father's possessions, (some of which were valuable) in a storage facility. Howard, with little outside access, save one friend of his, felt powerless. His lawyer was always busy. Eventually, Howard was notified that the monthly fee for the storage bin had not been paid in a while. Thus, there was to be an auction of Howard's possessions – personal, meaningful, and valuable.

In the meantime, Howard's son had hired a truck and tried to move Howard out of placement against his will in the middle of the night. Fortunately, the son was intercepted by staff of the facility who heard Howard protesting.

What happened to the thousands and thousands of dollars pilfered by the son? What happened to Howard's possessions?

Health Care Proxy

Similar to the POA, the health care proxy gives someone the authority to make decisions about the senior's medical care when they cannot communicate their wishes.

Sometimes the person who is designated to have Health Care Proxy is not the same as the one who has Power of Attorney.

The persons who are appointed POA and Health are Proxy must be able to work cooperatively when decisions must be made. While the health care proxy may make medical decisions the POA needs to be in agreement to pay for the medical care. If the two parties do not agree, decision making may be impeded at a crucial time and may have to be resolved by the courts. This could be a long and costly procedure.

Think of a situation where the person who is health care proxy is following the senior's wish to have all life sustaining interventions and the POA will not allow insurance to pay for them. Such a scenario underscores the importance of the senior making their wishes about medical care known and noted.

Guardianship

A guardian is a court appointed person who is responsible for the personal and financial affairs of the senior. The guardian is appointed when the senior is evaluated and found to be incapable of managing their own affairs. The definition of incapacitated is the inability to process information, evaluate information, and communicate effectively. Thus the person is deemed unable to make decisions about their health and safety. A guardian has more control than a power of attorney in making these decisions.

Anyone can petition for guardianship of another person. As such, they would serve as fiduciary for the care of the person and the management of their financial affairs. The guardian determines expenses to be paid for medical needs, the management of the estate, the handling of finances, income, and assets. The guardian gets a fee for their service.

The guardian has the responsibility of making an annual report or accounting of the senior's estate. The report describes the senior's needs, expenses, medical and psychological state, support systems, living arrangement, frequency of visits by the guardian, and the continued need for guardianship. Subsequent to the death of the senior, the guardian must submit a final report to the court within 60 days.

Wills

It is extremely important for seniors to have a will that is drawn up by a lawyer. The will specifies the senior's assets, possessions, and real estate, and how they want these things to be dispersed upon their death. It there is no will, and there are no surviving heirs, the State becomes the beneficiary of the estate.

A will should designate who will be the administrator of the estate. That person will be responsible for property distribution as specified in the will. Specifying property distribution minimizes the conflicts that can arise if the decisions have not been made.

Living Wills

A living will is a document which specifies what life sustaining medical interventions a person would like in the event they are critically ill and unable to express their wishes. Any competent person, at least 18 years of age or older, can make a living will. It must then be signed by two other persons, who are also at least 18 years of age. A living will (or advanced directive) allows a person to control and specify what medical interventions they would want under certain circumstances. This means the acceptance, rejection, or discontinuation of medical interventions. Such designations about which extraordinary measure are to be taken to prolong life, are called advanced directives. These decisions should be made when the person is capable of weighing the consequences. A living will requires that there is an individual who, if the senior is unable, will ensure that the medical decisions are followed in accordance with the expressed wishes of the senior. The living will goes into effect when an attending physician determines that a person is incompetent and in a permanently unconscious or incommunicado. The document becomes a part of the senior's medical record and cannot be changed without the senior's consent. Legally it is a crime to try to change someone's living will.

The living will accompanies the senior wherever they are located. It is standard practice for hospitals and facilities to have this document. The person who is designated to carry out the advanced directive has the responsibility for assuring that the hospital or facility caring for the senior has a copy of the living will.

Chapter 6
REMAINING AT HOME WITH SUPPORT

"I'm going home next week doc, so this is probably the last time we'll be meeting." Delight radiated from his face. He was a patient in a nursing home in the hills of northeast Pennsylvania. There, because he needed dialysis three times a week. His mood, now so upbeat, because he had found a way to receive dialysis at home.

Webster 1945, "home... one's own dwelling place ... the place or region with its familiar conditions or circumstances and associations...a place of refuge and rest...(page 190)"

Home is one's primary place for privacy and safety. A personal space where at the end of the day muscles relax and the bed feels good.

Lewis, a 73 year old man, was able to move back from assisted living in a suburb of Philadelphia to his own apartment.

"I thought life was over for me but that's all different now." He was assigned a caseworker who visited him on a regular basis and made sure he got to his medical appointments. He attended a day care center and then at the end of the day a home health aide cooked his meals and helped him dress and get to bed. "Life is still worth living," he stated. And this plan is less expensive than assisted living or a nursing home.

If you do your homework, you can find many creative seniors have found ways to obtain support and services without moving to a facility. An example of such is an option developed by

Reverend Kenneth Dupin, in Salem Virginia. In his travels throughout Middle Eastern countries he observed cultures in which elders were revered and lived in proximity to family. They were not seen as problems, as is often the case in the United States. His observations led him to develop a portable "MED Cottage." A 12 x 24 foot high-tech cottage with living quarters and a system to transmit the occupant's vital information to offsite caregivers. (www.aarp.org bulletin July – August 2010.) While not quite the same as living at home, it offers more independence and a safe environment where seniors can keep most of their possessions.

A recent AARP bulletin featured an article about a Philadelphia woman who moved out of a nursing home and returned to her home with the help of a counselor from the Philadelphia Corporation for Ageing and Nursing Home Transition Program. The counselor helped the woman organize all of her medical and financial information, set up a bank account, find a viable apartment, and find a home aide. In addition she received visits from a doctor who made house calls, she received weekly nursing visits, and got help with her grocery shopping from her daughter.

Most seniors state that they would prefer to age in place. They want to keep their possessions – the things that remind them of significant events in their life and define who they are. Seniors who require help with their personal needs would rather have support brought to their home than move.

A recent study by the Center for Medicare and Medicaid Services reported that less than five percent of the US population live in long-term care facilities. Even seniors who are disabled or who have a chronic illness prefer living in their own homes with support to living with relatives or in a facility. This is especially true if they are able to take part in events with family and friends, to do chores for themselves, and get outside by themselves.

Along with a growing trend to place seniors in assisted living there is also a beginning of a trend to keep seniors in their homes and essentially bringing assisted living to them. The Department of Housing and Urban Development is creating programs to keep seniors in their home. These programs cost Medicaid significantly less than what they would pay for placement in a facility.

In some states seniors who are eligible for government subsidized nursing care can stay in their homes with support at a considerable saving to the state. For qualified seniors services are provided through a waiver program. The waiver program frees up funds which would have been used for a nursing home. Eligibility is based on age, health status, safety factors, and the wish of the senior to remain in their home. In-home programs offer assistance with personal care, nursing care, therapies, medical supplies, and adult day care.

The decision for a senior to remain in their home should be based on an evaluation of their needs, and available resources, both people and agencies. This evaluation is largely based on how the senior is able to perform the ADLs (Activities of Daily Living). Additionally the number and types of support needed as well as the senior's physical and cognitive state determine whether living at home with assistance is an option and what services will be needed. If the senior has a permanent and progressive condition the feasibility of home care needs to be carefully considered. In these instances long range planning will indicate whether remaining at home will still be a better choice for the senior than relocating to a facility.

An innovative program worth noting is the "neighborhood village." It is similar to, but offers more assistance than, 55+ communities. The first of now more than 50 villages or pocket neighborhoods were started in the Beacon Hills area of Boston. Beacon Hills is one of the more than 50 nonprofit communities which provide services to seniors. Typically village members pay an annual fee averaging $600 - $1,000 a year for services such as transportation, managing finances, yard work, etc. Sometimes there are discounts for those with lower incomes. There are typically one or two paid employees who contact volunteers, contractors, community resources, and discount providers. The goal of the village residents is to stay as long as possible with the help of social support systems and from other village members. To find out about participating in or starting a "neighborhood village" system call 617-295-9638 or email: vtvnetwork.org.

Habitat for Humanity of Greater Charlottesville, VA, in cooperation with AARP Foundation (a privately funded foundation with the John W. Kluge Foundation) transformed a trailer park into 66 affordable housing units which the occupants rent and where utilities would never exceed one-third of their income. Almost ninety per cent of the families had a resident 65 years of age, or older. Sunrise Park, as it is called, is a community which offers guaranteed affordable living in which people can age well. There is a place for play (for children) and gardening and large porches, all of which work to prevent feelings of isolation. The AARP Foundation also works with other private foundations nationwide to help senior citizens. For more information, go to www.aarpfoundation.org.

Similar to the village concept is an organization called Life Force Foundation in Later Years. This was founded by a woman named Irene Zola as a result of her observation of her mother's struggle in a nursing home. She began the "Morningside Village" project in Manhattan, NY. It was the first non-profit sector of the parent organization Life Force in Later Years. Morningside Village connects frail seniors with volunteers who help them with activities such as getting to appointments, shopping, and meal preparation. Guidelines are available for setting up similar communities throughout the country by calling 347-688-6599 for information.

One of the most common reasons that seniors are moved to a facility is that they have fallen one or more times. As seniors age, the number of falls increase. Falls are the fourth leading cause of death for people between 65 and 85 years of age. The complications of falls include pneumonia, problems with circulation, and bedsores. Psychologically, seniors who have a history of falls, begin to fear that they will become more dependent and impaired. Emotionally, their anxiety and depression about this can make them unwilling to be active or to perform their ADLs.

The potential for falls and other safety issues, therefore, is perhaps the major factor for a senior being unable to remain in their home. Securing the home for the senior is a detailed process.

Assessing the seniors risk for fall involves answering several questions:

1. Have they had a fall or slipped more than once in the past?

2. Do they get dizzy when they stand up or when they first get out of bed in the morning?

3. Do their medications have possible unsafe side effects?

4. Do they have balance problems caused by muscle weakness, posture changes, decreased sensation and feedback from their feet, or changes in visions?

The following is a list of recommendations to reduce the risk of falls.

Clutter. In general, try to make the home as free from clutter as possible. Remove things that are lying on the floor, especially in narrow passageways, like hallways. Items that are lying around are hazardous. Mount loose cords and telephone wires to the wall and keep them out of the flow of traffic. Do not place cords under rugs or mats. Avoid having cords protruding from a piece of furniture where they may cause the senior to trip. Arrange furniture so that electrical outlets are close to lamps and electrical appliances. Move the telephone so that the cord is not in a place where the senior might trip on it. Consider using a cordless or wall-mounted phone. Ideally, there should be a phone in every room so that it is more accessible in the event of an emergency.

Lighting. Make sure all rooms are well-lit. Seniors loose visual acuity as they age and, therefore, need more lighting. Change to light bulbs that have a brighter output and install additional lighting where appropriate. Try to have furniture and rugs contrast with the floors so that they are more easily distinguished. Have light switches and lamps within an easy reach so the senior does not have to cross a darkened room to put the light on. Use night lights in the bathroom and hallways. Have a working flashlight at the bedside. Substitute to switch plates with contrasting color or "glow switches" to improve detection. Reduce glare by using frosted light bulbs.

Stairs, Hallways and Steps. These places pose a high risk for falls. Make sure all steps and stairways are even in their height and are covered by traction pads to secure footing. Place a visible strip at the edge of the step to delineate the steps. Make sure stairs and steps are well-lit, with switches at the top and bottom of the stairs. Handrails on steps and in the hallways should run the full length, so that the senior does not incorrectly judge the length of a staircase and miss the last step. Make sure the steps are in good condition and there is nothing placed, even temporarily, on the steps.

Floor Coverings. Make sure floor coverings are securely attached to the floor and that mats are not loose or slippery. Floor coverings should lay flat and not be worn or have holes in them. Use double-faced tape or a rug mat, if the flooring does not have a slip-resistant backing. Check flooring periodically for the need for replacement. If possible, replace shag carpets with low pile products which will not snag a cane or walker. Changes in surfaces between rooms are also a risk for fall. Therefore, try to contrast colors between rooms as a visual cue for the senior.

Bathroom. A great number of falls in the home happen in the bathroom. Hard surfaces and faucets present a risk for injury.

Sometimes, space restrictions do not allow for the passage of a wheelchair or walker into the bathroom. As a result, seniors will start to lean on towel racks or the sink for support. Make sure grab bars are available, especially for moving to the shower area. Grab bars should also be installed behind and on the side of the toilet. Adjust the handrail or bar to a comfortable height.

In the bathroom, faucets and door knobs should be easy to turn. To prevent scalding, set the temperature on the hot water heater to be no hotter than 120 degrees F. Raise the toilet seat to a height where the senior can sit with their feet on the floor. The seat should also be made from absorptive, soft vinyl to reduce the risk of fracture from sitting or dropping down hard onto a hard surface. Use skid-resistant mats in front of the toilet and bath. Mark the threshold at the doorway.

In the bath or shower, consider changing to a hand-held shower attachment, and provide a bench seat or stool. A liquid soap dispenser on the side of the bathtub or shower, or soap on a rope will decrease the risk of fall while reaching for the soap.

The bathroom door should remain unlocked so that the senior can be reached easily in case of a mishap.

Make Things Accessible and Easy to Use. Check to see that appliance controls and thermostats are easy to read and manipulate. Store frequently used things within easy reach so that the senior does not have to stand on a chair or step to reach them. There are numerous products, such as grab poles which help reach things. There are also special can openers and mobility products, such as canes and walkers, which can enable the senior to perform the activities of daily living.

Being in Contact. Place important phone numbers, in east-to-read print, near every phone. Consider having an automatic dialing system for frequently called numbers installed on their phone. For seniors with hearing loss, consider telephones with augmented voice levels, as well as door bells and smoke detectors with audible alert systems.

Improving Walking. Make sure the senior wears non-slip shoes with low heels and does not walk around in stocking feet, which may be slippery. Check to see that shoes fit properly. Encourage exercise, such as walking, to improve flexibility and strengthen the legs. Make sure clothing is not long, and does not drag on the floor where the senior can trip on it.

In Case of Fall. Have a plan rehearsed for what the senior should do in the event of a fall. Practice their lying down and using their hands to get to a piece of furniture which they can use for support. Practice how they can contact someone in case of an emergency.

Personal Response System. Monitoring of the senior's well-being can be arranged by scheduling volunteers, or friends and relatives, who check in by telephoning or by visiting the senior. For seniors who live alone, it is recommended that a 24-hour personal alert system be in place.

There are many companies that offer response systems. These companies have medical professionals on staff and keep a record of the senior's medical history. The system allows the senior to be in contact with friends and family for any emergency that arises.

Typically, response systems have three components. The first part of the system is a button that is part of a worn device or a speaker phone. Pressing this activates the second part, a radio transmitter connected to the telephone, which calls the response center or 911 (the third component). Some systems are set up to immediately send someone out if the button is pressed. This is a good option if the senior is unable to speak. The cost and ease of use of systems vary. Their options should be compared when selecting a system. Some companies offer coupons and other incentives. In addition to the safety factor provided by these systems, they increase feelings of comfort and security for the senior.

There are several other services which make it easier and safer for seniors to remain in their home. For a modest fee, there are telephone reassurance programs, usually manned by volunteers who check in with the senior on a regular basis. There are also programs run by local religious organizations, Senior Centers, and social service agencies which run senior companion programs. These programs have volunteers who visit home-bound seniors. The visitors observe how the senior is doing on an ongoing basis.

Working with Agencies. There are numerous agencies which offer an array of services for seniors in their home. Deciding which services are needed and from whom to obtain them can be daunting. Usually, it is easiest to work with one agency which can assess, obtain, and coordinate all the services a senior will need. These agencies may be public, private, or a self-employed person such as the previously noted Geriatric Care Manager.

As a rule, one should select a home health care service which is established, accredited, licensed, and certified to provide the services you need. Make sure it is Medicare approved and that its employees are bonded. Ask for, and check, references carefully. Find out how long the agency has been established in the community, and what is its reputation for quality and availability for services.

Optimally, one agency will be able to provide all or most of the services needed by the senior. These include skilled nursing, physical therapy, occupational therapy, speech therapy, nutritional therapy, assistance with ADLs, light housekeeping, meal preparation, shopping, laundry, continence care, help with ambulation, and help with transportation. In addition, some agencies provide assistance with medication, bill paying, and obtaining medical equipment.

A pivotal part of the services is the caregiver who will be going into the home. If the senior has a serious physical condition, such as Parkinson's or cancer, it is essential that the caregiver be knowledgeable about that disease. The advantage of obtaining a caregiver through an agency is that they must pass State and Federal standards to be certified.

Find out about the training and supervision of the caregivers. Does the same caregiver provide services for the senior on a regular basis? Families should get the name and telephone number for the person who supervises the caregiver. Find out how complaints are handled and what happens if things do not work out with a particular caregiver. Ask if there is a phone number where the agency can be reached at all times.

Working with an agency is a collaborative effort. The team includes family, friends, and the agency who work together to develop a treatment plan. The team determines whether the care is short term or permanent, and what services will be needed. Agencies are knowledgeable about what services a senior is entitled to, and are used to doing the paperwork involved in getting reimbursed for the services.

Some agencies require a minimum numbers of hours (usually 4 hours a day) for a health aide or nursing assistant, and a 24-hour day for a live-in companion. Some seniors only require a few hours a day or a few days a week, so it is important to match needs with the agencies requirements.

When working with an agency, designate one person as the primary contact and coordinator for giving and getting information. The primary contact gives information about the senior's needs, preferences, and personal likes and dislikes. Expectations about the caregiver's duties and any changes in the needs of a senior should also be specified. Finally, know who is in charge and who to contact if there is a problem or an emergency.

There are local agencies (County Offices on Aging) and Visiting Nurse Associations, and National agencies (The National Association for Home Care and Hospice in Washington, DC 202-547-7424, website www.NAHC.org), which provide a list of home-care agencies.

Hiring Home Care

Hiring a private caregiver means that the family takes on the responsibility of finding, interviewing, paying for, and coordinating services. The advantage of private hiring is that they may be less costly. In addition the number of hours can be tailored to the senior's needs. The family can also get a good sense of the fit between the caregiver and the senior. Caregivers hired privately tend to be found through the "grapevine", but can also be of high quality. A Geriatric Care Manager can be helpful in finding a qualified caregiver.

It is recommended that before hiring anyone, you set up a meeting in which you can observe how the caregiver performs the required services. Try to have someone else observing along with your during the interview. Do a background check. For a nominal fee, a law enforcement agency will do a check for history of theft or abuse. Observe the interaction between the caregiver and the senior to see if they are compatible. Obtain at least five references from previous jobs. Find out if there is flexibility in their schedule, and what is their back-up plan if they are unable to come. Can they provide back-up, or will it be up to the family? Seniors who have a caregiver come into their house to provide services must accept that a caregiver can do some things differently than they would. It is important that the senior and caregiver negotiate these differences to maximize the senior's comfort.

Make sure that the duties a caregiver is expected to perform are clearly explained and written down. The caregiver's responsibilities should be written down in the form of a contract. Family are likely to be responsible for overseeing that the services contracted from the caregiver are being performed adequately. Inherent in privately hiring someone for homecare raises the potential for a variety of problems. The caregiver may watch a lot of TV or you may be unable to get through because they are on the telephone. This may indicate that they are not adequately tending to the senior. There must be a way in place to track their reliability in terms of them arriving on time, and staying as long as contracted for. It is also important to look for signs that the caregiver is having visitors and therefore not spending time caring for the senior and for the possibility for the abuse of the senior; i.e., they may not be kept clean, they may not be thriving physically, they may seem fearful or upset with the caregiver.

It is further important to be aware of the possibility of theft from the home or overspending or misuse of the senior's money. The coordinator of the plan will have to oversee finances. In addition to monitoring the amount of money the caregiver spends, you will have to pay the caregiver and deduct taxes, Social Security, and half of unemployment insurance from their paycheck.

Payment for Home Health Care. It is probable that if the senior is requiring home health care, they will also need assistance with their finances. If the family does not do this, there are financial planners who can be hired to help seniors with their bills, checkbook, and investments.

Many families are disappointed to learn the limitations Medicare and Medicaid have for paying for services for seniors at home. Other sources of payment are private pay, private insurance, and some long-term care insurance policies.

Managing Money from Afar. Finances for seniors are becoming more complicated. Seniors have retirement plans, investments, bank accounts, and pensions with which they may need assistance. When families do not live near their senior relative, they may have to find someone nearby to oversee the senior's finances and be involved in money management.

Finances are a potentially sensitive area for seniors. Delegating financial responsibility to others restricts a senior's feelings about choice and independence. Seniors may also feel that this has implications about their mental abilities. It is helpful, as with any aspect of the senior's transition, to discuss with the senior what options will be best, especially before the need occurs.

Basically, the two choices when managing finances for a senior is for someone to take charge from a distance, or to hire someone who is located near the relative. In both scenarios, the person who takes responsibility should obtain a full accounting of the senior's assets and liabilities. This includes bank accounts, retirement funds, Social Security payments, pensions, investment accounts, credit card balances, mortgage payments and other debts. The responsible person should know where financial documents are kept and what bills are regularly paid.

If the family determines that they will handle the money from afar, a joint account should be set up for banks, stocks, pensions, IRA's, etc. Set up with the Social Security Administration to have the monthly benefits sent to you to be deposited into a joint account. Getting a debit or credit card for the senior to use for clothing, groceries, and necessaries, and have the statement sent to the family coordinator is a good way to monitor a senior's money. It is also important to regularly meet with the senior to set up a budget.

It is always advisable to obtain a durable power of attorney, which establishes the right to manage financial matters, if the senior becomes incapacitated.

If it is untenable to manage the senior's finances from a distance, there are professionals such as lawyers, financial planners, and Geriatric Care Managers who can be hired to manage finances. It is important to find someone who is reputable, honest, has references, and is professionally credentialed.

It is still necessary to oversee that person and be explicit as to what they should be doing regarding the senior's finances.

Obtaining Medical Services in the Home. In some communities, doctors, nurses, and medical students perform check -ups, do laboratory tests, and provide treatment for seniors who are homebound. This is both good preventative medicine and cost effective because it avoids repeated hospital visits by the elderly.

There are a wide range of medical services that can be provided to the senior at home. These include skilled therapies, such as physical therapy, occupational therapy, speech therapy, hospice, wound care, and medication monitoring. Skilled care and therapies must be prescribed by a licensed physician. The advantage of these services is that it allows the senior to obtain interventions and evaluations quickly before an illness becomes serious. Again, it is also cost effective, reducing the number of emergency room and hospital visits. The American Academy of Home Care Physicians, www.aahcp.org (410-676-7966) can help families find a physician who sees patients in the home. It is also important to try to work with a geriatrician, a doctor who specializes in the care of the elderly. The physician gathers information about the senior's social, emotional and physical condition. Their goal is to keep the senior as active as possible and slow down the ageing process.

Monitoring Medications. If a senior is not able to take their medications themselves, someone else must oversee this. The risk for seniors is that they will forget to take medications or will take inaccurate doses. For seniors who are still taking their own medications, dosages can be set up in the dispensers which set the time and dosage of medication. Some pharmacies will package medications in 30-day packets, by day, dose, and time. Some alert response systems will also call seniors to remind them to take their medication. Others have a programmed medication reminder that emits a signal which tells the senior to take their medication, and some provide a two-way communication system which makes it possible for the senior to check in.

Nutritional Needs. While seniors often look forward to meal times, it is not unusual for them to forget to eat or to eat something that is easy to prepare, but not nutritious. For seniors, this is a time when they are physically vulnerable. Therefore, good nutrition should include proteins, carbohydrates, vitamins, minerals, water, and fiber.

Some seniors lose interest in eating because their taste buds have diminished or they have to restrict their salt intake. This affects the palatability of food. Depression also affects appetite, even if nutritious, good tasting meals are available.

For seniors who are unable or unmotivated to prepare their own meals, many communities provide "Meals-on-Wheels". Meals-on-Wheels delivers two meals daily Monday through Friday – a hot meal for lunch, and cold meals for dinner and on weekends.

Transportation. When seniors are no longer able to drive or when there is no other transportation, some communities provide transportation services. These are often run by volunteers and charge a nominal fee to get seniors to their appointments, go shopping, and visit friends and family. Some transport services have vans which are wheelchair-accessible and some give a discount for seniors who frequently use the service.

Community Transit Agencies provide shared rides to seniors. The drivers are volunteers, there is a nominal fee, and advanced reservations are required. For a nominal fee, paratransit systems also provide seniors with rides to medical appointments, to senior centers, to grocery shopping, and other trips. Escort services provide transportation for seniors to social and recreational activities, volunteer employment, health programs, and educational programs. These types of activities increase the senior's social contact, improves their quality of life, provides them with an opportunity to feel useful, and decreases feelings of isolation.

Adult Day Care. Adult day care centers provide structured, supervised care for the senior during the daytime. They offer activities, meals, assistance with ADLs, medication administration, and an opportunity for socializing. They are an option for seniors who cannot be alone in the daytime, but who do have available caregivers at other times.

It is important to discuss the advantages of day care with the senior, as sometimes they may be reluctant to be away from the safety and comfort of their own homes. Explain the benefits of day care, especially if their physician has recommended it.

Day care is a place where seniors can get therapy, exercise, and monitoring of their health problems. They can meet and socialize with people who have similar interests. For many seniors, day care centers area a pleasant place for them to go for the day. This option allows the primary caregiver to have free time to tend to their responsibilities while knowing the senior is safe.

Day care centers are typically located in senior centers, churches and synagogues, and community centers. Many provide transportation to and from the center. Payment for care is usually by private pay, medical assistance, long-term insurance, private insurance, the VA, and the County Office on Aging. Because these centers vary widely, it is important for the family to do an in-depth on-site assessment of the facility. The center should have a program that meets the senior's needs, particularly if they have a special problem, such as memory loss, Parkinson's, or dementia. Therapists should be available to provide exercise programs and other therapies, such as physical and occupational therapy. Other services should include help with ADLs, continence care, medication administration, and blood pressure monitoring. Both indoor and outdoor activities should be available at the center. A good day care center offers activities that are challenging and which provide an opportunity for the senior to learn new skills. There should be small group activities which promote the formation of interpersonal relationships, large group activities, and individual activities.

The program that is developed for a senior in a day care center should take into account the medical screening and the information gathered in the social history. The Social Service Department at the center should communicate with the family regarding the senior's adjustment to the program. If the senior is found not to be appropriate for the program, the Social Services Department should help with after care planning.

In addition to an adult day care center, seniors can attend senior citizen centers where they can participate in activities and have meals. Seniors who attend these centers are usually higher functioning. Senior citizen centers offer educational classes, volunteer programs, and fitness programs.

Keeping the Dementia Patient at Home. Many families decide to keep the senior with a diagnosis of dementia at home, even as the disease progresses. Usually there is a primary caregiver who is responsible for the senior. To be the primary caregiver can be daunting.

Keeping a person with dementia at home helps them maintain their identity because the surroundings are familiar and their memories can be stimulated. The senior with dementia needs to be kept physically and socially active. Taking them for a walk, for example, is helpful when they are agitated or anxious. When their world becomes more confusing, and they become more disoriented, it is important to simplify their daily routine and structure their environment. This reduces the possibility that they will become overstimulated and agitated. Speaking slowly and calmly to them, and providing physical comfort, is also comforting. Make sure they have enough rest and allow for rest periods as needed during the day. If they are perseverative or agitated, it is helpful to call their attention to something else to distract them. Provide environmental and visual cause to orient them and minimize wandering.

The decision to keep a senior at home when they are suffering from dementia is a courageous one. Caregivers should make sure to make contact with their local Alzheimer's Chapter and include attendance of their support group in their schedule.

Caring for the Senior with Mental Health Needs. It can be difficult to obtain services for seniors who have mental health problems and are remaining in their home. Seniors who are developing a dementia may first present with confusion, forgetfulness, or disorientation. An early sign of dementia is difficulty learning new information. The above symptoms can also be caused by an infection, such as a urinary tract infection. When the infection clears, the symptoms go away. The persistence of symptoms though is suggestive of an underlying neurological problem. Additionally, problems with concentration and confusion may look like dementia, but actually may be a sign of depression, or be a reaction to a medication.

Seniors who present with withdrawal, agitation, sleep and appetite disturbances, and mood changes must be assessed by a psychiatrist for depression and/or anxiety. In some communities, there are day treatment programs for seniors with mental health problems. These programs provide psychological assessments, medication management, psychotherapy and family education. Often transportation is provided for the senior to get to and from the program. Costs may be covered by Medicare or Medicaid.

Unfortunately, many seniors with mental health problems are underdiagnosed or untreated. Their primary care physician may not specialize in, and may not identify or treat, psychiatric problems.

Some communities have "Wrap-Around Services" for seniors with mental health problems. Services are coordinated by an agency which develops a treatment plan with a caseworker. The caseworker assists the family in obtaining services, which meet the social and emotional needs of a senior.

Wrap-around programs are more cost effective when compared to institutional placement. They have the benefit of allowing the senior to remain in a home environment where they will be more comfortable.

Hospice. Some seniors choose to stay in their homes until they die. Hospice is a well-known national organization. Hospice provides in-home interventions for both the senior and their family when the senior has a terminal condition. They are well-recognized as being extremely skilled in providing psychological interventions to ease the pain, depression, and anxiety that accompany death. Hospice helps seniors deal with unfinished business and stay connected with their support systems. Family members who are responsible for making difficult decisions, such as advanced directives, and withholding treatment from a dying loved one, can be helped by Hospice in making these decisions. Hospice is noted for its assistance in enhancing a dying person's feeling of control and in preserving their dignity. Their reputation as a source of help is excellent.

One of the primary resources for seniors who remain in their home is the County Offices on Services for the Aged (COSA). They have considerable information about local resources.

Medicare and Medicaid are the primary agencies to contact regarding payment for services. Every state also has a Health Insurance Counseling Program which gives free information on health insurance and long-term care.

The U.S. Administration on Aging funds a referral service, called Eldercare Locator, which is an excellent resource for services (800-677-1116).

Chapter 7
MOVING

Leaving the familiar and loved, to move to some place new and strange, arouses anxiety. This is true, even if the senior has been part of the plan and believes it to be a good idea. The difference between what they had envisioned the move to be like and what the new life in fact is can be unsettling.

There is a scale of life stress events developed by Holmes and Rahe (1960) which is still used in research. On this scale, moving placed high on the list of stressful life events. For seniors a move, whether it be to live with relatives or to a facility, is likely to be their last move. While the move may be practical and even necessary, it can be a social and emotional challenge for the senior. It is not uncommon to be met with anxiety, anger, and distrust of those who suggest it.

The best scenario is one in which the senior has participated in the planning and has chosen an option with which they are comfortable. Having choices mitigates the stress of the move. Optimally, several choices have been considered, and discussed, even if the senior has objected and said that they are not ready to move. It is strongly recommended that discussions be initiated when the senior is competent and able to look ahead and make informed decisions about their future. The worse-case scenario is when the senior has no input and is unexpectedly manipulated into a move.

> *Robert: He reasoned. He pleaded, he even cried. He was fearful for his mother's safety but she was staunch. She wanted to stay in her house with her things, her kitchen, her bathroom, porch, and bed.*

She told him her plan: Sonny could do this, Margaret that, and so forth, and she would be all right. But the family did not think it would work and it was decided that Robert would be the primary mover.

Finally one day he convinced her take a ride. She did not know that there was a suitcase with her belongings in the trunk of the car.

They passed "The Place" and he said, "Let's just go in and look." "NO! I don't want to. Let's go home." She was afraid, she did not know the place and her skin felt cold, then hot and flushed. He said: "This is the best place for you."

She was so afraid, her heart beating, feeling trapped, paralyzed. "No, take me home." Crying. He cried too.

A long awful time parked in front of "The Place." After some time she quietly said" I have to go to the bathroom." He said "I will take you inside and we will find a bathroom". And that's how they walked in.

For seniors who move, it is a time of paring down and living in a more restricted space. Giving up the comforts of their home and parting with meaningful possessions echoes losses of the past. Being relocated without having a chance to choose what they will take with them is like being robbed. Remember that our possessions are a part of us. They are part of our comfort and identity. Having to part with them is like giving away part of ourselves. Parting with items that were associated with a loved one, diminishes the ability to preserve part of them. It is important to be sensitive to even the small things that matter to seniors. Make sure that they bring along photographs, their bedspread, their favorite chair, and portable things that they did with their leisure time. Look through clothing with the senior and select items they like as well as items that will be practical.

Make sure they have comfortable, practical shoes. Do not bring valuables, as they have a way of disappearing even in the most upscale places and even places which say " We have no stealing here"(!!!!!!!!!), Provide toiletries that will last at least two weeks and provide snacks that the senior enjoys.

In addition to making sure that the senior is able to bring along items that are meaningful, try to find a way to preserve their former routines and contacts. The routines in facilities are structured and not always flexible. Work with staff to try to keep aspects of the seniors routine intact. It can be reassuring for the senior to be in touch with their former community-- their friends, church, physician. Make sure these people know where the senior is going. Arrange it so that the lists that were made of important documents are safe and that they are available to the senior upon request. Give seniors the list of names of their support network, including friends and agencies. Decide what they can still manage on their own (*i.e.* ADLs, medications, finances).

When it comes to the actual move, seek help in packing and moving those items that the senior has selected. The spares them the stress of having to watch while some of their possessions are left behind.

Accompany the senior to the facility and help them set up their living space in a way that is comfortable and perhaps closely approximates how things were set up in their home. For example, was the bed near the window, or was a table near the window?

On the day of the move, remain with the senior and accompany them to their first meal in the facility. Make sure that they are settled in and then take leave without a tearful adieu.

Aside from the practicalities of the move, the schedules, new people, and new environment are a source of upheaval. Again the senior may feel anxious, lonely, and fearful. If the family is not sensitive to their complaints the senior may feel abandoned. Complaints should be acknowledged, not dismissed, while encouraging the senior to find a way to deal with the new challenge themselves.

For many seniors it is difficult for them to start again. They are reluctant to try to form new relationships which can end in loss again and which are not as close as the relationships they have lost. Physical or mobility problems may become an excuse for them to stay in their rooms. They may need encouragement and assistance to go to activities and to leave their rooms at mealtimes. Initially the family can ease the stress by spending time with the senior, helping them to become familiar with the physical layout of the facility, and going to a few activities with them. Ask the staff to encourage the senior to try to go to activities.

It is not unheard of for seniors to resist the move, particularly of it was not of their choosing. If the family spends time with them and encourages them, their period of adjustment will not be as long.

Once the senior has settled in, the family should try to insure that the living arrangement remains stable. Incompatibility with a roommate (when room sharing is necessary) may indicate a need for change. Sometimes the senior has to move to another room or even to another facility. Remember though that each time a senior has to move, even within the facility, they are traumatized. Therefore good planning should anticipate a senior's long term needs.

Lastly, a senior may request a move to another facility. For many reasons the facility may not be best in terms of the "goodness of fit." The seniors' request may therefore be valid. Exploring this possibility will give the senior the feeling that they can be heard, can make decisions, and have control over their lives. If the move has to be made on the basis of financial limitations, the senior will again be stressed. This again highlights the importance of planning ahead. Seniors today are living longer than in the past. When looking for a facility, take a long-term look at how far finances will go. Work together to find a place that will work for the long run. Research has shown that the mortality rate is higher in seniors who have to move again than in those who don't.

Seniors in transition are like cut flowers separated from their roots. Put them in a well–lit place, free from temporal winds, and well-watered, and they will retain their petals for a while. But the more you move them around, the more tenuous their attachments to the stem and the faster the petals fall. While you can maintain the bare stem for a while, it has lost its essence and its sense of what made it special.

Chapter 8
EVALUATING A FACILITY

Sophie was having more trouble getting around her house, even with a walker. Grocery shopping by herself had become nearly impossible, because even the few steps in and out of the house required a lot of coordination.

She sighed, took her time. She wanted so much to manage because the space for her had opened up at the assisted living facility. Sophie had her husband's pension, Social Security, and a little money saved, but she worried about money. Mostly she loved her home and did not want to leave.

Convinced by her daughter to "just look at the place" again Sophie had agreed and had gone to see to the large high rise facility, where residents took elevators down from their rooms to the dining room level and where she soon might live.

Sophie was not familiar with elevators. Her daughter said, "You will get used to it. There is always someone there to help". Sophie was afraid the elevator doors would close on her walker.

At the assisted living high rise, she looked at the room. One room. Where would she put her things? What would she do? There was so little that would fit. Her cups and saucers! Her sofa!

For the senior who can no longer remain in the home, or live with family, the option is to move to a facility. The goal, in medical terms, is to find what is called, "the least restrictive setting". Translated into laymen's terms, it is to find that place which provides the care needed, but also allows for the most independent functioning. In addition to being "least restrictive", there should be a "goodness of fit". This means the matching of the senior and the facility in terms of level of care, homogeneity of population, comfort level in terms of ambience, types of amenities, proximity to former relationships, and ability to pursue interests.

It is a paradox that, as we get older, we are less adaptable to change and it is at this time of life that we are confronted with so many changes. Moreover, for each individual, there is a limit to the amount of change that can be tolerated without the senior feeling that they have lost their life. This is sometimes manifested by the senior's inability to adjust to the new environment.

To minimize the possibility of an attenuated period of adjustment, the senior and family should explore options well in advance of when they will be needed. This will avert having to make a quick decision.

While convenience is often a high priority, it should not be tantamount to a senior's happiness.

> *The resident was an unhappy 70ish man who had been relocated from his apartment in the Midwest to be close to his daughter who lived on the east coast. She placed him in an assisted living facility, but did not visit often. He missed his girlfriend who was back in the Midwest. He was in good health, except that he suffered from extreme back pain due to arthritis in his spine. He was very unhappy, frequently grouchy, unapproachable, and difficult to engage in conversation. His back pain, at times, prevented him from getting around independently. He stayed in his room most of the time and was in the assisted living facility less than six months before he died.*

Before visiting a facility, prepare questions and then make notes during the visit. Initial impressions are important when you walk into a facility. Is the first impression one of being hopeful, or hesitant and/or reluctant? Can you say to yourself, "I could live here"? Would you like to spend possibly the rest of your life in one of the rooms, be comfortable in the bathroom, and be satisfied eating the food every day?

Visit as many facilities as possible and pay attention to your instincts. Your visceral reaction is as important as the features and amenities you will be shown.

A good source of information is someone who has a friend or relative who is a resident at the facility. They can give you their impressions, experiences, and information.

In your first visit, you will meet with the administrator who can tell you about the history of the facility. Ask how long has it been in existence. What is the financial status? Is there a waiting list? How long has it been owned by the same company? Is it the first venture of an independent developer, or part of a regional or national corporation? Ask to see recent assessments, inspections, and licenses. If the facility is not licensed, do not consider it. Ask to see the most recent evaluations by State and Federal agencies. Take the tour and listen to the formal presentation the first time you visit. Then narrow your choices to two or three possible facilities for more in depth evaluations.

The in depth evaluation is the time to assess the staffing pattern. Find out who is in charge. Does the staff seem friendly and knowledgeable, or stressed and disinterested in the residents?

Talk to the residents, find out what they like and dislike about the facility. Sit with the residents at meal time. Get an impression of the mealtime ambience and the quality of selections on the menu.

Ask to have a copy of the contract, in order to take it home review, so that you can ask questions or take it to a lawyer who specializes in geriatric law. Examine the contract. Inquire about the responsibilities of the family and those of the facility. What are the rights of the residents and how are grievances handled. Is there an advocate for the resident? Ask what conditions or behaviors may result in a resident being discharged and what are the policies about decisions to leave either by the family or by the facility.

Read the most recent inspection and licensing report. Find out whether deficiencies have been corrected.

Some facilities have formal treatment plans for their residents. This is more often found in nursing homes, than in assisted living facilities. If a facility has treatment plans for its residents, ask who participates in the development of the plan, how often it is reviewed, and if the family can participate and have input into the plan.

The People in Charge

The administrator of the facility is the most important staff person. Their responsibilities are to make sure the staff are doing their jobs and that the residents are well taken care of. The administrator is the hub of the wheel that makes the facility run smoothly. They hire and fire staff, manage the various departments, determine salaries and budgets, make provisions for staff training, and determine job descriptions. They should be visible to staff and residents.

Meeting with the administrator tells you how much they know about all aspects of the program and how well they know the residents. If the administrator cannot meet with you, rule out the facility. Ask how long the administrator has worked at the facility and what their employment background is.

Administrators vary widely in their skills. There are those who are truly hands on and available and other who rarely peek out of their office. There are responsible, ethical, and caring administrators, and negligent, and fraudulent administrators. The following is an example of the latter.

An article in the Philadelphia News, April 2010, reported about a head of a personal care home in Pennsylvania. She had appropriated the residents' Social Security checks for herself. She continued to cash their checks, even after they were no longer living at the home.

At her trial, the defendant bared her head to reveal that she was receiving treatment for cancer. She then took out her teeth to display that she had dental problems. The court actually subsequently gave her a verdict of leniency (due to sympathy).

But what about the seniors she had swindled? Where was the leniency for them!

The Line Staff

The disposition of the staff and how they relate to the residents is crucial to the senior's adjustment. It is difficult for seniors to give up their independence and have to rely on caregivers. It is demoralizing and demeaning if the resident feels beholden or fearful of staff. Or made to wait, or not be taken seriously, or to be treated brusquely.

***Sam** could always be found sitting quietly in his recliner, moving as little as possible, to avoid the jabbing pain in his back, that accompanied most movements.*

From the comfort of his chair and blanket, he loved to reminisce about his days in West Philadelphia and the small jazz band he played with. He had few visitors, except for a daughter, who visited at least once a week. At times, he seemed to be in more discomfort than others, but he was not one to complain. It came as a surprise, then, that he quietly alluded to the fact that he was not being treated gently by staff who helped him dress and undress. Upset, but wary about divulging this, he told his therapist that one staff in particular was always running late in getting the residents ready for breakfast.

He then demonstrated. "She takes my arm and shoves it into my shirt, sometimes bending it and making me hurt". Always soft spoken and wary, but obviously distressed. Wanting help with his plight, but fearful of making trouble, less the aide find out and be retaliatory with him.

The aide who helped him dress for bed could also be brusque, however he would allow his complaints to go no further than his room and the therapist, and thus thwarting attempts to help him.

Residents encounter a variety of staff during the day – cleaning people, personal aides, and dining room help. Many of the staff are paid at minimum wage and have taken the job out of need, rather than inclination. They are not caregivers by nature and are vulnerable to burn-out.

Making a left out of the elevator, there was a large cleaning cart blocking the hallway.

"Excuse me", the therapist said, on the way to seeing a patient. Only to be met by a barrage of profanity from the woman whose cart it was.

A turn to the right instead to another patient's room.

Once there, "Who is the cleaning lady on your floor". "Oh, that's Gloria. You don't want to mess with her", was the reply. "Why? What is she like? What is her name?" "No, no, Dr. B. If she finds out that I've told you about her..., please don't say I said anything."

At the nursing station, a question asked about the cleaning woman on the sixth floor elicited a response from the head of maintenance department. It was that Gloria was "sort of" on probation. Fortunately, this inquiry resulted in her being fired. But what if it had been a chance turn to the right, instead of a left, out of the elevator?

To those staff who find themselves unhappy and frustrated, the recommendation is," find someplace else to work". This suggestion is made because caregivers are often a substitute or the closest thing to family a senior has. To depend on someone who is resentful or disinterested is demoralizing for the senior.

It is helpful when evaluating the staff, to find out who the contact people are for different aspects of the program (i.e., medical, food services, activities, financial, etc.). Try to meet with these people. This would give you a heads up of who to contact, should a particular problem or question arise.

Try to observe whether the staff treat the residents with dignity. Do they knock on their doors before entering? Do they insure privacy in the bathroom? Do they speak to the residents in a caring manner? Are they patient? Are call bells answered promptly? Are the residents dressed, clean, and well-groomed? Are the staff careful not to embarrass or criticize residents, either publicly or privately? Do staff understand that there are different approaches for different residents?

What is the staffing pattern of the facility? In addition to the director, is there an activities director? What is that person's experience and training? Is there a social service director who is aware of special concerns and issues for the resident? This person should work with the staff and help the residents with their initial adjustment and at other difficult times. The social service director also is the contact person for the family when something needs to be communicated.

Find out the ratio of staff to residents for each shift. How many levels of care are available in a facility? Do staff really encourage residents to go to activities, take them outdoors, and bring them in again when needed.

Staff training has a direct relevance on resident care. Training provides staff with updated information and helps prevent burn-out. Find out what kind of in-service training the staff get and how often. Do they know how to do CPR? Can they establish continence programs for seniors who need it? Are they trained to deal with wandering and aggressive behavior? Do they receive special training to recognize dementia and psychological problems? What is the turnover rate for staff? What is their average length-of-stay on the job?

Again, try to spend the time talking directly with staff. Your instincts about staff, in addition to the answers to your questions, will provide you with valuable information.

Medical Staff

Find out what medical staff are available and what services are included in the monthly fee. Is there an additional charge if medications are administered by the staff? What medications can be given out without additional charge to the residents?

Is there a physician who consults to the facility? How often does the physician see the resident? Is the physician available for special visits, as well as routine visits? Can the residents keep their own physician and, if so, is transportation provided to the doctor for them? Does the doctor have adequate time for each senior, or is there a long list of patients they have to get through in one day?

The good practitioner asks questions about the patient's mental and physical condition and checks with the nurse to make sure the dosage of medication is appropriate. Some seniors, whether at home or in a facility, continue to have the same prescription refilled month after month without ever being seen by the prescribing physician. The physician should be looking for drug side effects, drug interactions, and the efficacy of what is being prescribed.

> *A relatively high-functioning patient in an assisted living facility suddenly started complaining to his psychotherapist about feeling dizzy and confused. His therapist checked his chart and found there was a mistake. He was being administered ten times the prescribed amount of Prozac. A staff-frenzy ensued and the prescribing psychiatrist was quickly contacted.*
>
> *Staff blamed each other; but fortunately, the patient had spoken up, and the error was corrected.*

What kind of ancillary medical services are provided? Do physicians, therapists, psychologists, podiatrists regularly see the patient? Is there speech therapy, hearing and vision assessment, and dental services? Is hospice accessible when needed? Who determines the need for special services – the facility, the family, the senior?

Nursing Staff

Most facilities have a nurse available during the day. Ask if they are a registered nurse, an LPN, or an unlicensed person, who has the assignment of giving out medications.

Is nursing care available 24/7, or only daytime? Who is responsible when the nurse is not there? What are their qualifications and what procedures are in place, should a medical emergency occur.

There is a very attractive assisted living facility in South Jersey. The nurse's office is actually overstocked with personnel, but the door is usually closed and residents sit outside in a line of chairs waiting to be seen. The number of staff in the office has NO correlation with the speed with which are seen. By way of contrast, there is a family-run assisted living facility in Delaware County, Pennsylvania. The nurse's office door is always open, except when she is out checking on a resident. The nurse does not need to be updated on the status of a resident, their mood, whether they are eating, or are having family problems, because SHE KNOWS.

Nursing staff should be sensitive to a resident's complaint, whether it is convenient or not.

> *Bess, who had lived in an assisted living facility just over a year, developed a painful ingrown toenail. The podiatrist, who came to the facility every six weeks, cut her nails, but in the interim, the nail had grown back and was again in-grown. Bess suffered with a condition that required special medical attention, and which did not get better with the care she was receiving. She applied cotton balls and Witch Hazel, limped to meals, and kept her foot elevated – to no avail. The floor nurse was contacted. Her response was that the podiatrist would be back in three weeks and that the resident always complained about her toe. Well, of course, that was true, because she was in pain. But Bess was in pain and felt demeaned. She was afraid to "make a fuss" because she was concerned that she was asking too much and the nurse would get angry.*

Ombudsman

Ask if there is an ombudsman for the facility. An ombudsman is a member of the community who has no political or financial ties to the facility. Their role is to advocate for the residents, and they should make themselves available to residents who have concerns. Some facilities have no ombudsman; some have one who rarely, or never, shows up. Some ombudsmen who do show up have meetings with the residents, but allow staff members to be present!!! Facilities who do have an ombudsman are obliged to put their name and contact information where it can be seen. In some facilities, the notice is quite small and inconspicuous. In the initial orientation, mention is made of the existing of an ombudsman, but in the hustle of the resident moving into the facility, this can be forgotten. Some ombudsmen make themselves very obvious and involved. They can be a valuable advocate for the resident.

Food

For many residents, mealtimes are the highlight of the day. Mealtimes should be a time of socializing and having an appetizing meal. The ambience and the comfort of the dining room contribute largely to the enjoyment of eating. Ask whether residents have assigned seating or can they choose with whom they want to sit. Are seating arrangements changed, if a request is made? What efforts are made to introduce a new resident to the dining room for their first meals? Residents almost always report that this is an awkward time. Facilities should have a plan for welcoming residents and making them feel comfortable.

Ask who does the cooking. Is there a chef on staff or is food brought in from a food service? Does a nutritionist or a dietician review the meals? Ask to sit with the residents at mealtime during your visit. Take note of how the food tastes and how extensive the food selection is. With age, the sense of taste diminishes. It is therefore important that the foods are seasoned and well-prepared. Seniors are used to their own food choices and cooking. They should have a sufficient variety of selections so they will be able to find something they will enjoy.

See how long it takes for residents to get their food, or cup of coffee, and whether the kitchen runs out of things. What is the atmosphere in the dining room? Is it quiet and restrained, or do the residents engage each other in conversation? Do staff go through the dining room, making contact with the residents? Are there snacks and decaffeinated beverages available to the residents throughout the day? Are there restrictions on visitors bring in food? What provisions are made for special dietary needs? What arrangements are made for having a tray delivered to the resident's room? Is there a charge for this and when is it an option? Ask for the residents' opinion about the food.

Transportation

Seniors in facilities depend on others for transportation. Find out what provisions are made for transportation to medical and other appointments. Is there a fee for transportation? Are the vehicles used by the facility wheelchair-accessible? Is there public transportation nearby, and are residents allowed to us it?

Stealing

"Stealing does not happen here." That is what you will hear from the person who tours you in the facility.

> **Bess** *was dressing for the Christmas holiday. She wanted to wear her favorite Christmas pin. She checked in her night table to find it was gone; the same night table from which some cookies and socks disappeared. Socks walk in facilities!*

> *When in her distress, Bess complained to the Director of the facility, it was pointed out to her that, in fact, she had her Christmas pin. "No, no", she cried to deaf ears. "I had two pins, and the one I really like is missing".*

*Session 3: **Don** is talking about the loss of his wife and two adult children. His son died as a teenager in a car accident and his daughter died of breast cancer at age 52. Clearly he struggled with unresolved grief issues and now felt the loss of the relationship he had with his second wife. When they had met, he had been lonely – missing so many people he had lost. They had gotten along pretty well. But, now he reminisces. He reports feeling lonely and put upon. The sound of his wife calling his name, "Don, Don", rankles him. He is though, responding well to problem-solving sessions in which he comes to see that some time out of their room by himself does him good. His only reprieve had been taking his car to run errands midday, and now he realizes that there is no reason to stay in the room just to be nearby his sleeping wife.*

Occasionally then, he goes to a planned activity where he is well-received because he is caring and congenial.

*Session 9: Again depressed, **Don** had been weaning off his anti-depressant medication, but now presents with more frustration and gloominess. His appetite has decreased and he visibly appears to have lost weight. He does not like taking medication for anything and is even stoic about taking his Percocet, prn for pain. He depends, instead, on an extra-long time in his morning shower to allow the warmth of the water to penetrate his aching back and knees.*

Now he is nostalgic about his youth and early life. He speaks of growing up and eventually running a farm of his own. He had loved caring for the animals and raising crops. For him and his first wife this was a good life and now he is nostalgic. He feels disconnected, dissatisfied and must be convinced to again to increase his medication and allow himself the intermittent activities which bring him some pleasure.

Session 14: **Don** *moved to an assisted living facility, because his wife no longer could remain at home. While at one time, she had been pleasant enough, she now was again very demanding and Don was often at her call. "Don, Don", his wife called again. She seemed to call his name for everything. He was again so frustrated and haggard. He was a truly kind and competent 90-year-old. Except for severe arthritis in his back and legs, (for which he took his Percocet) Don was generally healthy. Being cognitively clear, he was able to manage his own medications and drive a car. One day, he thought he noticed some Percocet tablets missing from his bottle. He told this to the head nurse. When he noticed that half of his Percocet refill was missing, the nurse in charge became alarmed. The first response was that Don was told he could no longer manage his own medications. The second response was they called in the local police, because Percocet is a controlled substance. The police did an investigation and, subsequently, a staff member was found guilty and fired.*

Session 18. **Don** *was still upset about the incident with his Percocet when he went out one day at noon to do an errand. He left a note on his door for his therapist. On this particular day, he learned that his favorite lunch, liver and onions, was being served. He asked that the cook save him some for when he returned. The cook replied, "No problem". Don returned, checked with the kitchen to be told, "Sorry,* *we forgot and threw out the rest". Don, now quite upset, made a fuss. To which the cook replied, "Wait a minute, I'll see what I can do". What Don observed the cook DOING was taking some liver out of the trash, dropping it on a plate, and bringing it out to him.*

In anger, Don ventilated to his therapist. More frustrated than before, he said he wanted to move to another facility.

*Session 24. In time, **Don**'s wife became more disabled and, eventually, hospice was called in to care for her. Hospice, however, did not come on the weekend, and Don wanted to make sure that his wife had some kind of a bath. He removed his watch and ring, so that he would not scratch her, and placed the ring inside the watch on his night table. The watch had little value; the ring was a Mason's ring with a diamond – a beloved gift from Don's first wife.*

Don and his wife went off to lunch. Lying down for a brief nap after lunch, he turned to see his watch on the night table, but....no ring. Panic, disbelief. He jumped up, looked behind the night table, under the bed, all over. He thought how strange, how could it be, did the ring jump over the watch? Looking all around, even in impossible places.

A call to the Administrator, "Did you look behind the table and under the bed". Usually calm, Don is now agitated, angry. He gets no support and, in fact, is left feeling that the Administrator implied that it is his own neglect. He grieves his loss. He is sure the ring was stolen, and ventilates to his therapist. He is more determined, now, to move to another facility, although it is impractical.

Moving to another facility will not assure that there will be no frustration. "Stealing happens just about everywhere", his therapist explained.

The next week, the head nurse greets the therapist, advising that the facility will be hiring an alternate therapy person. She also notes that the family had decided that Don cannot benefit from therapy any longer, because he gets confused, like when he thought someone was stealing his Percocet. "But you called in the police, and fired someone", the therapist said. "If you had a problem with something I said, you should have come to me", said the therapist. "No, no, we just want to give the residents choices", said the nurse. Out the front door and back in again. "Well, here's how it will go", said the therapist, "I will finish seeing my current patients, but I will not be taking any more consults from you".

Some months later, while visiting the facility to see a private patient, who had just been moved there the therapist asked "By the way how is the alternate therapist working out?" Nurse: "Oh that never came through. They just could not find time to come in".

***Claire**, a woman with moderate to severe Parkinson's disease, moved to a high rise assisted living facility in the suburbs of Philadelphia. She was reclusive and depressed – embarrassed by her illness and somewhat abandoned by her family who could not bear to watch her decline. She tended to get irritated and agitated easily and, for this reason, she had a "testy" relationship with several of the staff.*

One day she received a call from her credit card company questioning charges amounting to almost $5,000. She was extremely alarmed, knowing that she could not possibly put these charges on her card.

Agitated and upset, she called the administrator of the facility who first asked her if she was she sure she had not made the charge. Alarmed Claire was unsure what they would do to help.

When she calmed down, Claire resolved to do some investigative work herself. She figured out who and when someone could have had access to her card. The cleaning person was confronted by the administrator and subsequently fired for theft, but not before Claire had felt frantic and unsupported.

Call bells are lit at the nursing station near Grace's room. A visitor called the nurse's attention to the buzzing sound they are making. Aides and nurses are shuffling around, seemingly impervious to the sound. The buzzers had been going off for some time. The visitor points to one and said, "That one has been buzzing for ten minutes". The nurse, irritated with the buzzer and with the visitor, states, "She always rings like that. We get to her as soon as we can. It's usually nothing". She knows they don't answer the buzzers quickly enough. They are stretched thin. Sometimes patients are not put on, or taken off, the bedpan in a timely fashion. They complain. They are more uncomfortable than they should be. The nurse is caught between defending the staff and being annoyed at a situation for which she feels responsible.

The patients are in good spirits today and so are the staff. Today, an antiques dealer is coming to the nursing home to run an activity which is similar to the "Antiques Road Show". Residents and their families are encouraged to bring in items, either from their homes or from their rooms, so that the appraiser might discover a "find" for them.

Grace keeps a small old Bible on top of her dresser. She thinks the cover might be ivory, but it is actually, plastic. At the nursing station, the buzzer goes off and there is a commotion in Grace's room. They hear her wail, upset as they flip off the buzzer and rush to her room. "They took my Bible, someone took my Bible". Her breath is coming in shallow gasps. "Bible is gone. Nothing to show." The nurse begins, "Maybe you put..." But then, stopped. She realizes that Grace is wheelchair-bound and cannot lift herself, even to transfer in and out of bed. "Maybe your daughter..." "No, no." She knows the small Bible had been in the box on the dresser. "Grace, Grace". The nurse tries to comfort her. She likes Grace, who is always appreciative of the help she receives. "Grace, we will look for it".

Look where! Small Bible clearly stolen, although the facility does not acknowledge that stealing ever takes place. Clearly gone! Taken probably by someone who lived or worked there. The best they can do is to try to persuade the tearful Grace to go to watch the "Antiques Road Show" activity.

Stealing does happen and it is a cruel assault on the senior. In the paring down of possessions (a necessary part of moving to a facility), there is so much that is left behind. Things accumulated over the years with associated memories and comfort from that which is familiar.

It is astonishing, the things that are stolen from the senior's room, and the denial and dismissiveness of staff - loose change, cookies, pairs of new socks, a sweater, soap, a credit card.

If your loved one complains about something gone missing, don't raise an eyebrow immediately, or ask them if they looked all around. Be the advocate. They may not live with you, but it is still on your watch.

To facilities – be kind. Think of how fragile you feel when you can't find the one thing you were looking for. Imagine looking and looking, then being sure it was stolen, or thrown out by someone else.

Chapter 9
ALTERNATIVE LIVING ARRANGEMENTS

55+ Communities

Fifty-five plus communities are the least restrictive setting for seniors who want to downsize and want to live with a more homogeneous population of people their own age. These homeowners are still active, independent, and some still work or have special interests, such as doing volunteer work, or participating in activities which meet regularly.

These communities vary in their physical structure (from apartments to individual homes), as well as in the available amenities and maintenance fees.

What distinguishes 55+ developments is the sense of community that exists between residents. Typically, there is an openness and friendliness between homeowners and a readiness to help each other. There are ample opportunities to form meaningful relationships and to socialize at activities and in clubs.

In deciding on a 55+ community, important variables are location, type of dwelling, cost of housing, and maintenance fees.

Retirement/Continuing Care Communities (CCC)

Healthy active seniors may also choose to buy into a continuing care community. These communities provide a full spectrum of levels of care, from independent living to skilled nursing. All levels are in the same geographic location.

To be accepted into a CCC, the senior must be in relatively good physical and cognitive condition. They are typically mobile, able to drive, and may still be working. There is a "buy-in" cost, which essentially equals purchasing the "luxury" that as their needs increase, they will be able to stay in the chosen setting, where they can receive all levels of care.

Similar to a continuing care community are planned adult retirement communities. These offer a transitional step from total independence to an environment in which some care and amenities are available. Some planned adult communities have onsite medical facilities.

The minimum age requirement for admission to a continuing care community is 62. Typically there is a substantial monetary buy-in and monthly fees, which cover housing, services, and nursing care. Seniors pay a high entrance fee for a long-term contract which allows them to move through the levels of care for the same initial monthly fee. Contracts vary so that if the senior leaves or dies, sometimes the entrance fee is refundable, or partially refundable. An alternative payment option is a "fee-for-service program" in which fees are added as additional services and care is needed.

A life care community is similar to a continuing care community, but it requires a higher entrance fee and does not charge additional fees as the level of care increases.

Continuing care communities are attractive because of the amenities they offer. These can include housekeeping, meal plans, transportation, fitness centers, activities, outings, on-site beauty shops, banking, 24-hour skilled nursing, convenience stores, conference rooms, on-site entertainment, gift shops, wellness programs, and business and computer centers.

The disadvantage of these types of communities is their costs and restrictions. Entrance fees can be high and not refundable. The monthly rental or mortgage must be paid, even if the senior goes to the hospital. Also, unlike living in one's own home, there may be restrictions regarding visitors, pets, who can use the facilities, and the vehicles that residents can have.

The ability to pay is an important consideration in choosing a life care or continuing care facility. It is important to understand the different types of contracts and refund policies.

Types of Contracts. The Extensive Contract. This type of contract has the highest entrance fee, but covers housing, residential services, and unlimited nursing care with no increase in payment as more care is needed. The Modified Contract. This covers housing and a specified limit on nursing care. Once this limit is reached, additional care must be paid for by the resident at a daily or monthly rate. The Fee-For-Service Contact. This type of contract has the lowest entrance and monthly fees. It includes housing, use of the amenities, meals, housekeeping, transportation, and short-term or emergency nursing care. Long-term nursing care, though, must be paid for by the resident at a daily rate. It can be provided in the resident's unit, or in special rooms designated for personal care. Life Care With Equity. This is a very expensive option. The resident buys a unit, owns it, and can sell it, if they wish. To buy into these facilities, the senior must meet stringent physical and financial requirements. Despite this, there are a large number of financially secure seniors who choose this option. Consequently, these facilities often have a waiting list, and even require a fee to be placed on the waiting list.

Before selecting a community, check to see that it is accredited and find out what is provided at each level of care. Consider the location of the community. Is it near friends, family, shopping, and physicians. Consider the ambience and what is provided. Ask the question, "Do I want to live here for the rest of my life?"

Assisted Living Facilities

Marilyn stated, I can't take care of her anymore. I can barely take care of myself. We never really liked each other. She came here because of Tim. It's too much for me.

*Surprisingly, **Theresa** does not seem overly upset about the prospect of moving to assisted living. She had generally liked getting out of the house to go to the day treatment center when she was less depressed. The prospect of going someplace does not faze her.*

They visited a small family-run, well-regarded facility in Delaware County, Pennsylvania. The administrator is welcoming. She speaks to Marilyn, to Theresa's older son and, at length, to Theresa. She does not talk down to her. She is interested in Theresa and they have a common Italian background. She takes time to show them all around. Theresa can have her own room. She can bring her furniture (although she actually will opt to bring very little of her belongings), but this does not make her unhappy.

Theresa meets the nurse, the activities director and the owner. She sees a lovely dining room. Nothing is off-putting or distasteful. This will be alright.

Theresa is less depressed than she has been in years. She and the administrator have bonded. The staff and other residents like her. She is poised, polite, and sweet. Plenty of food - ice cream twice a day if she likes, activities, (if she wants - - sometimes, she goes). Mostly, she likes the bigger events where everybody attends. Her older son brings her a cup of coffee every morning. The other residents see this and it makes her feel special. She does not care if no one else visits, although her daughter and granddaughter do visit regularly.

Theresa is stable for some time — a few years in assisted living. She is, though, beginning to have some memory and balance problem. She has had a fall. She has some medication changes. Her mood is stable. She does not incur a diagnosis of clinical depression, but she has a habit with is off-putting to the staff and other residents. She picks her nose and throws it on the floor.

The owner of the facility cannot have this. It is a health and sanitation concern, and source of complaints.

At the suggestion of the therapist, a private aide is hired to do some behavioral training, as Theresa is having some memory problems. The aide is supposed to work on behavioral interventions, but for all intents and purposes, is useless. She does not check in with the therapist, and does really nothing, despite being paid by the family. Theresa continues to "drop" on the carpet in the hallways.

The owner is unhappily considering asking the family to take Theresa elsewhere, but then comes up with the idea that, perhaps, Theresa could get more care in their dementia unit. At first the family is put-off. They feel that Theresa is not that cognitively impaired, but they do not want to start looking around again.

The Alzheimer's unit is cheerful, nicely decorated and well-staffed. The rooms are bright. The food is fine. Theresa is not consulted. She is moved. She is a bit confused about it, but once there, does not seem to mind and is again well-liked and not depressed. The staff report that she has not completely stopped her habit, but it is accepted as part of someone who is becoming cognitively compromised. This is a good outcome for Theresa.

__Sophie__ remembers always feeling special and expecting "specials." She was the youngest of four children and adored by her father. Pretty, petite, curly blond hair, blue eyes. *As a young woman, she had many suitors, but she chose Sol.*

"Why Sol?" her father asked. "Because I like to dance, and he takes me out when I want." She was never really sure if Sol liked to dance. She thought though that he probably did not like it as much as she did. After he died, she suffered guilt about him, wondering if she had cared enough and been sensitive enough to him. Sometimes, Sol would balk when she would tell him they were meeting another couple to go dancing. But she would always be busy worrying that they would be late, and they always went.

In assisted living, she cried to her therapist about her fear of going to hell, because she had not been kind to Sol.

In the morning, she had her routine. She would get up late, thus missing breakfast, and then had to do her make-up routine. She had cajoled the staff to bring her breakfast. Cereal, raisin toast, and coffee. Then she had time to primp. She did not appear before lunch. She is an exception to the rule. The rule is, meals in your room only when you are ill. But Sophie finds it difficult to maneuver her walker into the elevator to go downstairs for meals. She has, therefore, prevailed to have her "specials" and her leisure.

Sophie pushes the chair back from the table, tries to step.

Da dada dada da da.

Stars shining bright above you

Da dada dada.

..whisper I love you

But in your dreams

whatever they be,

dream a little dream

of me.

> *Sophie tears up. She is depressed and lonely, having somewhat alienated the one friend she had made in assisted living. She sometimes has problems with sleep and tends to be over-reliant on Xanax, which her physician keeps trying to reduce. She is, though content in her routine in her room. From her vast collection of 50 years of stuff, she has moved with her furniture (her couch, table, chairs, and bed), her cups and saucers, purchases from thrift shops and consignment stores, gifts from friends). All cherished. Much left behind. She has brought her wedding pictures in a silver frame, which she looks at and gets sad.*
>
> *She sleeps in most mornings and watches Turner Classic Movies till late at night. No need for an alarm clock. She has a leisurely life.*

During the past more than ten years, assisted living has been used by caregivers as the answer for seniors who can no longer live on their own. There has been an enormous proliferation in the number of assisted living facilities built.

For some seniors, assisted living may be the option of choice, but for others, it is a difficult change in lifestyle.

Actual quotes from seniors in assisted living:

- "It's not that it's not a nice place, but it's not your life"

- "The big decision of the day is what to wear"

- "All my life I did what I wanted and I got what I wanted. This is ridiculous"

- "Stealing. Oh, yea, they stole my socks, my shorty pajamas, my extra toothpaste and toothbrush:

- "It's difficult. You went to church. You made your own breakfast"

- "The goal is to try to make a life"

- A petite 93-year-old woman says, "I'm very careful about voicing my opinion here, because I don't want to eat it later"

- One senior stated, "I walked into the lunch room for the first time. I felt like a non-person. Everyone said, 'you can't sit there, and you can't sit there. That's Jack's seat'. They're all cliques. I got a seat and said to the people at the table, "they should give people numbers for the seats". A lady at the table said to me, "NEVER sit here again". I was afraid to tell my family that I was unhappy. I thought it would put them off and they had helped me. It made me feel more alone not being able to talk to them about how I felt.

Unfortunately, too often it happens that the senior is left out of the decision-making process. The family and the facility make decisions, even though the senior is still cognitively capable to know and express their wishes.

Families who are considering assisted living should first contact the National Center for Assisted Living, 1-202-842-4444 or www.ahcancal.org/ncal. They provide a list of licensed facilities and regularly review them. They also have information about the facilities' staffing requirements, medical services and contact person.

Assisted living provides 24-hour supervision to people who need help with personal care, (such as bathing, dressing, toileting, housekeeping, meal preparation, taking medications, and basic nursing care). Seniors who cannot live alone, but do not need the degree of care provided by a nursing home, are encouraged to function more independently in assisted living.

Assisted living facilities vary widely in the number and quality of amenities they provide. This is reflected in the quality at mealtime, in activities, in gathering rooms, in health and fitness programs, in scheduling of room cleaning, in laundry service, and transportation. Some facilities provide dining rooms or places where residents can entertain guests. Some have a more homogeneous population and a separate part of the facility for dementia patients.

The quality and availability of medical care also varies. Some facilities have a nurse available 24 hours per day, while others rely on nursing care via telephone contact in downtime, such as evenings and weekends. There is usually a physician who comes in once a week and is available to residents who do not choose to remain with their prior primary care physician. For those residents who do keep their primary care physician, there must be a way that they get transported to appointments and a way that the facility keeps in contact with the primary care physician, as well as, other medical specialists.

Many assisted living facilities also contract with independent professionals, such as podiatrists, physical therapists, and psychologists who come in to see residents on a regular basis.

In addition to the basic amenities, a good assisted living facility has a recreational program which offers activities that are more stimulating than bingo, arts and crafts, and movies.

As a rule, the more the facility provides, the higher the monthly fee.

Advantages. More than one million seniors, mostly women, move to assisted living facilities. They are usually mobile, active, and enjoy outings. They live in either private or shared rooms, depending on their preference and financial ability to pay for a private, rather than shared, room. For some residents, the company of other seniors and the activities are a buffer for feelings of loneliness and isolation. This is especially true at mealtimes.

Safety is the main reason for moving from home. The advantage of on-site healthcare promotes the feeling of security.

Disadvantages. Unlike nursing homes, assisted living facilities do not have to meet requirements for Uniform State or Federal Accreditation. For this reason, it is important to check licensing or registration by the State.

Assisted living has become a sophisticated business. Most facilities have public relations departments with skilled sales people and attractive brochures. They assure that they can meet the senior's needs and keep them happy. Nonetheless, residents report that their adjustment does not match what the brochure suggests.

Fees. Financial arrangements also vary widely from one facility to another. In some, there is a monthly fee that covers basic services. Additional services such as bathing, administration of medications, and assistance with dressing incur additional charges. Facilities that charge higher monthly fees will usually provide more of the additional services in their monthly charge. Because monthly fees may escalate as needs increase, it is important to try to consider future, as well as, current needs.

The cost of assisted living is usually covered by private pay, as health insurance and Medicare do not pay for custodial care. Some residents have planned ahead and have long-term care insurance which covers some of the costs. Sometimes VA benefits also pay part of the costs. The downside of the cost of assisted living is that private resources are exhausted and assisted living does not have Medicaid beds, the resident will suffer the unsettling and re-traumatizing experience of moving again.

Personal/Residential Care.

Sophie moves to Personal Care

Sophie had established a routine for herself in assisted living. She liked to stay up late watching old movies, and sleep late in the morning. Despite complaints about pains in her arms and legs, her depression lifted. But now Sophie is out of private funds and must move again. The money she had sheltered by "gifting it" to her son is gone. He had spent it on himself, and now has no way of reimbursing her. Her daughter confronts the son to no avail.

Sophie cannot stay in assisted living. She must move across the street to a personal care facility which is situated in the basement of a nursing home. The facility is gloomy. One corridor, dark gray rugs, and about eight rooms on each side of the corridor. A very "basic" dining room with bland meals. There is no room for her kitchen set, her bookcases, her many possessions. She brings her recliner and her couch. They provide a single bed. There is no nurse. Mrs. Buelly, a rather large cumbersome woman is in charge. Her mood is often gruff (she has her own physical problems) and she has low tolerance for residents not doing things exactly her way. She is intimidating. Mrs. Buelly does not approve of Sophie's routine. She does not like that Sophie wears a housecoat, stays up late, and wakes up late. She insists that Sophie dress for breakfast, and she lets it be known that residents must "do for themselves". Sophie feels that, at this time in her life, she should be allowed the simple choices about her daily schedule. She resists.

Mrs. Buelly has taken an adversarial stance vis-à-vis Sophie. She makes it uncomfortable for Sophie. Sophie has also become mildly incontinent of urine and Mrs. Buelly threatens that if Sophie does not comply with her rules, she will have her moved to the nursing home. She will have to get up for breakfast and go to bed early. Sophie has already scaled down *twice – once when she moved from her home to assisted living, and then when she moved across the street, from assisted living to the basement. She feels threatened.*

Seniors who cannot care for themselves, or have extremely limited financial resources, may need to go to a residential care facility. These are typically multi-unit apartment complexes. They must be licensed and provide a protected environment. They provide personal care for a small number of residents and usually provide at least one meal daily.

In contrast to this, personal care homes are privately owned homes which provide the senior with room and board, cleaning, laundry, and assistance in taking medications. Help with ADL, such as bathing, dressing, and personal hygiene are not routinely available. Personal care homes need not be licensed, and therefore, they may be more lax in how they are run and what they provide. Because they do not have to meet government standards, conditions at these homes may be less appealing and substantial. Medicaid may not cover payments for them if the conditions in the home are substandard. The absence of standards and evaluations opens the door for unsavory conditions and even neglect and abuse.

Advantages. Personal care homes have the advantage of providing a more intimate home-like environment. The smallness and closeness of the setting (which is often a house) encourages socialization and friendships.

Disadvantages. These homes are for residents who are mobile and do not have major limiting conditions. There are no medical resources in the facility, but personal care homes are usually in neighborhoods where the residents have access to medical services. Sometimes the manager of the home will help with the administration of medications. Typically, there are no planned activities in these homes and the residents watch TV or can go out for walks. There are shared or private rooms, and shared bathrooms.

Costs. Personal care homes have a monthly rental fee. Some have an entrance fee, which may or may not be refundable. Entrance into a personal care home does not require the disclosure of one's finances. These boarding homes vary widely in their costs, appearance and how they are staffed. In selecting a personal care home, make sure rooms are large enough, especially if they are shared and that there are enough bathrooms.

The residents should be dressed, groomed, and cognitively homogeneous, as some personal care homes accept seniors with cognitive impairment, while others require that residents be alert and oriented.

Watch for signs that the residents are over-medicated, in restraints, or not dressed. The absence of required reviews and regulations leaves the door open for verbal, physical, and financial abuse. It is not unheard of for owners of these homes to appropriate and misuse senior's assets and Social Security payments. Be prepared that, for many reasons, such as changes in the senior's physical or cognitive state, there should be a backup plan to move elsewhere.

Nursing Homes.

Mrs. Buelley Wins

Sophie had to move upstairs to the nursing home part of the facility. Mrs. Buelly finally had her way. Sophie has to give up all of her belongings. Her table, lamps, pictures, trinkets – everything that fit in her room, but not in one-half of a hospital-type room.

She shares a room with a semi-conscious woman who moans most of the day and night. She now has only a wheelchair, some pictures, some clothes, and a TV. Emotionally, she is depressed and distraught. She has a mild case of incontinence, which results in a faint smell of urine. Sophie, who has always been meticulous about her person, is self-conscious and embarrassed.

Sophie's urologist tells her that she is a candidate for corrective surgery that will shore-up her pelvic muscles. While this has the possibility of resolving her problem, Sophie is fearful of surgery. In the meantime, Sophie's daughter is very supportive and has been able to get Sophie onto the waiting list of an excellent facility in the same county. This facility has a chapel where Sophie can attend services. She eager to move and the daughter works on the move when she has time.

As the result of her depression, a psychiatrist was called in to evaluate Sophie. She has expressed the desire to die, and join her husband. Sophie is diagnosed with major depression and is medicated with Zoloft (a popular anti-depressant). Months go by with no progress on the move to the new facility.

Sophie's therapist visits the new facility and was told by the director that Sophie is not a priority for admission. Although on the waiting list, priority is given to patients who are being discharged from hospitals or are coming from home. Since Sophie is already in a placement, she is not a priority. If, however, she was being released from a hospital....

The family and Sophie's therapist discussed the recommendation for the incontinence surgery and the benefits both for her physically and for her getting into the other facility when released from the hospital. Sophie is interested now. There is a way. She called her daughter to start the process.

The director at the nursing home, however, hears about the suggestion of Sophie's therapist and decides that the therapist was no longer allowed to see Sophie.

It is explained that, although she has been seeing Sophie, as well as other patients, since the transfer from assisted living, she is not an actual consultant to the nursing home. The therapist requests an application to be a consultant, but was denied. Sophie is assigned a social worker with whom she does not relate well. There will now be no leaving her shared room, no move, no hope.

A nursing home is a facility for people who need 24-hour care, but do not need to be in a hospital. Residents of nursing homes typically have significant medical problems and, in the nursing home, they can receive long-term, short-term, rehabilitative, and acute care. Often they are coming out of the hospital and cannot return home. Some will never return home.

Care is provided by registered or licensed practical nurses, and there is supervision of one or more consulting physicians. Physical therapy, speech and occupational therapy, psychotherapy, and units that provide ventilators and tube feeding are often available and are paid for by Medicare or Medicaid.

While there are nursing homes that do not deserve the gloomy reputation they have had, residents generally agree that it is a depressing way to live out their lives.

Many nursing homes make efforts to enhance the lives of their patients. They bring in music therapy, pet therapy, religious services, amenities such as beauty parlors, and a variety of medical consultants. They are also better regulated than previously, but patients still often live in cramped, shared quarters where their call for assistance with the activities of daily living, as well as basic needs are too often left waiting. This is disturbingly uncomfortable and demeaning, as nurses are at times impervious to the sound of the call bell, either because they are under-staffed, or just become numb.

Nursing homes simply do not always receive enough government or private funds to balance their budgets. Studies have shown that nine out of ten nursing homes are under-staffed, and that staff are under-paid and do not receive the crucial training and support required to work for the very needy population.

Reports by the AARP found a high percentage of nursing homes continued to have deficiencies which are serious enough to endanger patients. There are reported incidences of negligence and rough-handling, bordering on abuse. Additional deficits can be noted in cleanliness, the occurrence of bed sores, quality of food, use of restraints, and the overuse of medications to keep patients sedated and quiet. Some medications have serious side effects when used over a long period of time. This is more apt to happen when the physician does not regularly evaluate the medication, but rather just re-writes for the prescription.

For years, the FDA has warned that "off-label" use of antipsychotic drugs has resulted in significant side effects, such as hallucinations, aggression, sudden cardiac arrests, stroke, and significant weight gain. The FDA has suggested the use of medications, rather than behavioral interventions, has contributed to higher death rates in seniors on these medications, than in a matched control group not on the medications.

Nursing homes are a clear reminder of progressive illness and death. As such, it may be difficult for patients to ward off depression, maintain positive self-esteem, and feel that they have a purpose in life. Their high need for physical care underscores their lack of independence and power. It is not unusual for them to feel that they have to stay on the good side of their caregivers, or risk insensitive brusque care.

Marie-Pherese Connolly JD, a prominent and accomplished lawyer in the field of elder abuse, has reported a four-fold increase in mortality rates, disease, and injury as the result of elder abuse in nursing homes. Elder abuse is defined as neglect, physical, psychological, and sexual mistreatment.

Families who try to intervene and advocate for their loved one may find themselves face to face with some harsh, restrictive realities. They may be identified as troublesome and interfering. If they complain about the facility, they may find their visiting rights restricted, even to the point that they may be banned from the premises. The facility may be able to obtain a temporary restricting order. While there are some families who are irritating, and felt to be over-critical, preventing the patient from seeing family is a serious issue. Imagine a frail senior unable to be in contact with family, and family unable to see whether detrimental or neglectful conduct is being covered up while the loved one deteriorates. The pluses and minuses of some nursing homes are improving considerably, but others may be becoming more retaliatory, poorly staffed, and neglectful

Advantages. The main advantage of a nursing home is that patients can receive the medical care they need without having to be in a hospital.

Disadvantages. The move to a nursing home means that a person will have a minimum of personal space and possessions, and that their stay is likely permanent. Their surroundings are extremely restricted and they are usually cut off from the outside world. Visits tend to be short, as nursing homes are depressing places to visit. The cost of care in the nursing home is very expensive; therefore, it is worthwhile to consult with reports by the AARP that some seniors can get the same services in their own homes at the same or less than the cost of a nursing home.

When evaluating a nursing home there are considerations beyond those typically made at other facilities. One is the condition of the residents. Nursing homes, by their very nature, care for an impaired population. In view of this it is important to observe if residents look like they are being made comfortable. Who is the ombudsman? Contact him. Does he visit at regular hours? Can he describe the strengths and weaknesses of the facility? Are residents' needs attended to in a timely fashion? Are call bells repeatedly not being answered? Obtain a copy of the most recent inspection?

Nursing homes, unlike assisted living facilities, are required to have a treatment plan for the residents. These are reviewed on a regular basis. Both the family and the resident have the right to attend and participate in the development and review of the treatment plan. Therefore, they should be advised of the date of the review. Patients and families should have access to medical records. For residents who are cognitively intact, participating in the treatment plan increases their sense of control and purpose. This also bolsters the feeling that they have not totally relinquished decisions about their lives.

Residents of nursing homes are people with rights. Their complaints may come from adjustment issues, anxiety and depression. However, their complaints may also be reality-based and require that the family intervene and advocate for them.

Patients in nursing homes have the right to some privacy – optimally to have time alone in their rooms, especially if they share a room, as is often the case. They certainly have the right of privacy in the bathroom. The exception to this is, if there is significant risk for injury in the bathroom. They have the right to privacy during their telephone calls, during times with visitors, and with their mail.

Costs. Basic nursing home costs (which are usually based on a daily rate), include room, meals, housekeeping, general nursing care, recreation, and personal care. The facility must specify services and fees in writing. Medications and special therapies are usually not included in the basic rate, nor are special equipment and laboratory services. Amenities, such as TV, telephone, and beauty care also usually have an additional fee.

Payment for nursing homes is by private pay if the facility is not regulated and certified by the State. Some facilities accept

Medicare for the first 20 days, but then require a co-pay from the subscriber. There are strict requirements before Medicaid takes over payment. Families are encouraged to "spend down" in order to become eligible to Medicaid. The parameters for "spending down" are very strict and families are encouraged to adhere to requirements. This is best done with legal advice.

Not all facilities have Medicare or Medicaid allotted beds. Find out if Medicare or Medicaid beds will be available if private resources are exhausted. Look into the feasibility of obtaining long-term health insurance as early as possible, because insurance premiums increase if they are started later.

If the resident and/or family exhaust their private pay resources, the senior will have to move again, which is not a good experience.

Information about what Medicare and Medicaid will pay for in a nursing home can be obtained from your State Health Insurance Assistance Program.

Resources for information about nursing homes including the following:

- Internet site, *www.medicare.gov/nhcCompare/home*. This compares nursing homes on several dimensions. Also go to the web site, *www.medicare.gov* and clinic on State Survey Agency and State Health Insurance Assistance Program.

- *www.hcta.gov* is the website for the Medicare Health Care Financing administrator

- *www.medicare.gov/nursing/overview.asp* provides publications such as Nursing Home Compare, "Your Guide to Choosing a Nursing Homer" and "Alternatives to Nursing Home Care"

- *www.aoagov/default.htm* is the site for the Administration on Aging. This provides many resources

- *www.aahsa.org* is the website for American Association on Homes and Services for the Aging

- *http://www.aarp.org* is the site for the American Association of Retired Persons. This provides a wide range of information of services.

- *http://www.jeffdanger.com*, on this site, click on Elder Care Consulting: The Truth About Nursing Homes. This provides information about many subjects related to nursing homes.

Alzheimer's Unit.

Theresa has Alzheimer's. She moved to the Alzheimer's unit and has her own room. It is sparsely furnished. That is how she has chosen it to be, since moving from Marilyn's house.

Daytimes are spent in the large activities room where there is always something going on. Theresa has her set seat, where she can always be seen in a circle of residents. She participates marginally, but is always there to listen.

"How did you find me?" is her typical greeting to the therapist she still recognizes. "You know, I will always find you," is the answer that makes her smile.

But now, she is having some episodes of combative behavior, which really do not respond to medication changes. She can swing at a staff for no apparent reason, or for some minor frustration. More medication is not an option. Theresa has shown considerable slippage over the years and behavioral problems, which do not respond to interventions, do not make continued placement a viable option.

Theresa must leave. She is quite frail, confused and, except for the routine she has followed for years, cannot really incorporate new information. She cannot stay. Another place that would accept her must be found.

Alzheimer's Units are specialized separate living quarters, sometimes in the same building as an Assisted Living facility or nursing home. They are set up to care for patients who are confused, disoriented, and have memory problems associated with a dementia. These are secured locked units. There should be a high staff-to-patient ratio and staff should have special training to meet the needs of a senior with dementia.

Oftentimes, families resist placing their loved ones in an Alzheimer's Unit. They do not seek placement until they are physically, emotionally and financially drained. In reality, it is preferable to move a senior to an Alzheimer's unit when they can still learn to find their way around and become familiar with the facility, staff, and routine. Researching an Alzheimer's unit should begin when early signs of dementia appear. This will allow that, when the loved one needs placement, there will be a plan. Many units have a waiting list and may Alzheimer's Units prefer to take their patients from the Assisted Living or nursing home with which they are associated.

Advantages. The main advantage of an Alzheimer's unit is safety. The setting and structure prevents the senior from wandering off and engaging in behaviors which could be harmful to them. The staff in these units are typically more tolerant, trained, and able to care for seniors with dementia. For the family, moving the senior into an Alzheimer's unit can relieve some of the stress of trying to care for someone with a progressive challenging illness.

Disadvantages. Moving in itself is a disruptive experience. For the senior with compromised cognitive ability, moving is even more confusing and anxiety-arousing. It is difficult for people with dementia to incorporate new information and learn to find their way around in a new residence, with new people, and new routines. Separating them from family is especially anxiety-arousing. A senior who moves to an Alzheimer's unit needs a lot of support. People with dementia live in a world which progressively becomes more confusing and unpredictable.

In many instances, Alzheimer's units are depressing. Some facilities do not invest in making the unit as attractive as they would if they had to please a more cognitively aware population. It is not unusual to see a difference between the Assisted Living part of the facility and their Alzheimer's unit in terms of décor, furnishings, attention to detail in the dining room, and menus at mealtimes.

Being in an Alzheimer's unit can be stressful because other residents can wander into the senior's room, take their belongings, call out repeatedly, and become aggressive to staff and other residents.

Costs. Costs at all types of facilities keep rising. In comparison to in-home care with a senior with dementia, an Alzheimer's unit can cost four times as much. Private pay is still the major source of payment. Private insurance typically pays for acute illness, but not for the long-term care required for an Alzheimer's patient. Some long-term care insurance policies will pay for care, but the policy must have been purchased before there were any signs of dementia. The amount paid and duration of payment varies between policies.

Families should check Social Security Disability Insurance, Supplemental Social Security, Veteran's benefits and State funds. As of 2002, Medicare began to pay for several services needed by Alzheimer's patients. However, payment is still unsure for skilled nursing care at homes, but not custodial care, and not care in a facility. Some long-term care facilities accept payments from Medicaid, but not many beds are available for Medicaid patients.

Information about financial help can be obtained by contacting the Elder Care Locator Service (800-677-1116).

Reichel, William (Editor Emeritus) Reichel's Care of the Elderly. Clinical Aspects of Aging. 5ᵗʰ Ed., Baltimore: Lippincott, Williams and Wilkins, 1999.

Roiter, Bill. Beyond Work. *Ontario: John Wiley & Sons, 2008.*

Romano, Joseph L. Legal Rights of the Seriously Ill and Injured: A Family Guide. *PA: Joseph L. Romano, Esq., 2011.*

Simpson, Carol. At the Heart of Alzheimer's. *Gaithersburg, M.D: Manor Healthcare Corp., 1996.*

Thayer, Jane and Thayer, Peggy. Elder Essence: The Gift of Longevity. *Maryland: Hamilton Books, 2005.*

Chapter 10 THIEVES and SCAMMERS

There are thieves and there are scammers.

Seniors can be the victim of both — victims of their families and in the world at large. Over 90% of financial abuse of elders are actually committed by a senior's family members -- children, siblings, grandchildren, nieces and nephews, etc.

For families, money and valuable items are the object. Remember Pearl was the victim of Ivan, Sophie lost her $10,000 to her son, and also the man in assisted living, whose son had Power of Attorney and took the proceeds from the sale of his father's condo, and emptied his father's bank accounts.

There are thieves (sometimes petty thieves) who try to obtain a senior's belongings (jewelry, computers, flat screen TVs). They usually have an accomplice with whom they gain false entrance to the house.

A duo can come the seniors 's house offering a free appraisal of the roof, appliances, or a service. They knock on the door. The senior (used to being gracious) lets them in to do their estimate. They case the house and one of them takes something or, sometimes on the date of service the senior allows them in to do the work and they do their job--- they rob.

If you receive a phone call from a number you don't recognize and you answer and they hang up, someone may have just been checking to find if you are home before attempting a break-in.

In senior facilities, employees, who usually are paid poorly, may steal to augment inadequate wages. Betty lost her favorite Christmas pin. Don lost his Masonic ring. This might be considered "petty thievery," but is devastating for the senior.

Scammers are people who try to get your personal information and use it to get money. They are not interested in family heirlooms, jewelry, or a TV. They want money and they can be pretty slick about getting it.

It's highly probable that a senior has been approached by a scammer by phone, email, or via a radio or TV offer , or an advertisement posted somewhere soliciting a product or service. Seniors are twice as likely to be scammed than members of the population in general. Why are seniors targeted more frequently?

Seniors often have good credit and financial savings.

They tend to have more health issues. This makes them vulnerable to promises of cures and products which can miraculously improve their health. These are usually offers which traditional medicine does not make.

Seniors are offered products and services which will make their activities of daily living easier. Seniors are often home to receive calls from scam artists and cold calls. Their loneliness and tendency to be polite make it more difficult for them to hang up the telephone.

They may not live close enough or be in regular contact with a family member with whom they can discuss a potential fraud.

Seniors tend to not report suspected or actual frauds because they do not know where or to whom to report them.

Scammers know that seniors may not immediately realize they have been defrauded .They may have difficulty recalling details of the fraud which reduces the likelihood of a successful investigation. The statistics associated with senior fraud are astounding.

The AARP estimates that $400,000 billion dollars of telemarketing fraud were perpetrated on seniors .These schemes include false sweepstakes, telephone offers, offers for credit cards, and offers for work done on their homes.

The average cost for senior losses from home improvement fraud range from $1,000 to $5,000. Seniors have also lost an estimated $500 million aa year from forged checks. Over $14 million dollars of internet fraud was reported 15 years ago (way before the internet became so central to households). Most of the$14 million was lost on online internet auctions. How much has that number increased to in 2015?

Healthcare and equipment expenditures are estimated to be more than $1 trillion a year. Ten percent, or $100 billion dollars are lost to fraud. * Estimates of successful scamming of seniors have been as high as $36 billion dollars. What is even more disturbing is that once a senior has been identified as a successful victim of a scam, there is an escalation of scammers who approach them. There is network of scammers who notify each other of the senior's vulnerability.

Phone/Telemarketing Scams

A telemarketing scam may begin with the scammer calling and telling the senior that they represent a service or business that the senior used before. The scammer will take advantage of the senior questioning their own memory and not being sure if they, if fact, had previously ordered the service or not. Therefore they end up signing up "again". But it is a scam.

Telephone scams are the most notorious (even exceeding internet) scams perpetrated on seniors. Typically they are offers which begin with, "You've been selected" to receive a certain product, and advised to act quickly in order to take advantage of the offer. The elderly are particularly targeted for this.

Seniors are offered prizes, lottery winnings, travel packages, easy loans, requests to contribute to a special charity, and so on. The goal of the scam is to get the seniors bank account and personal information including credit card numbers, bank account numbers, birth date, debit card numbers, and Social Security numbers.

Fraudulent telemarketing scams are successful with the elderly because seniors are less mobile and are used to shopping by telephone. These scams that occur over the phone they are difficult to trace because there has been no face to face or paper trail to follow.

Phone rings. Dr.B. "Hello" Caller. "Hello, Aileen."

Dr. B. "Who?" Caller (with foreign accent) "Aurnee?"

Dr. B. " Who is this?" Caller : "This is Luis"

I am calling you to give you chance to _____"

Dr. B. "NEVER call this number again." Hangs up. Then thinks about it to self." Crud, missed a chance to hear a scammer in action." So I checked Caller ID. It's France Bernardo (this is the 5th time the number appeared on Caller ID. 1-805-614-9665).

I Called the number and got "We are sorry. The number you have called has been disconnected or is no longer in service." Such was the case with about a half dozen other unsolicited calls in the previous 10 days.

Frederick Williams 1-215-738- 8832. (Does not exist)

Green. 1-864-663-1110. Not a real number.

Neither was Rockwell, Texas. 1-215-771-7003.

Or Fort Lauderdale. 1-954-358-4855, or Salt Lake City, Utah. 1-801-410-7837.

Scammers are pretty slick because they cannot be traced. It is likely that all seniors who call their Caller ID will find a half dozen calls in the preceding 10 days that are likely unsolicited scams.

> **Phone rings**.
>
> Dr. B. "Hello"
>
> Caller " Hello, (can't remember if he asked for me by name or asked for the head of household).
>
> This is Holimer (or some difficult to understand name) from One (something)
>
> Dr. B. "Who?"
>
> Caller:' Hollimer (accent difficult to understand), from One Step_____'''
>
> Dr. B. "Hollywood, who'"
>
> Caller (Just a tad exasperated) ".Oliver, Oliver James from One Step_____"
>
> Dr. B. " Can I get your phone number?"
>
> Caller" Click. Hollywood Holimer hangs up.

Beware of the scam which offers a huge foreign lottery prize. Soliciting by telephone or mail is prohibited in the United States and purchasers rarely get the lottery ticket.Lottery and sweepstakes scams often come in the mail. Typically the senior receives a packet that claims to be from Reader's Digest or Publisher's Clearing House. This sweepstakes directs the senior to deposit "the enclosed check to their bank account" and then wire a part of it to cover fees for the transaction. The check bounces but the senior loses whatever money they wired to the scammer. These fees can be substantial. Furthermore once the scammer learns the senior's bank account number and it can be shared with other scammers.

Unsolicited extended warrantees are also offered by phone and mail. The scammer will find out the make and model of the appliance, heat/air conditioning unit, and most often, car. The warrantees do not come from the vendor or manufacturer. The senior gives their money to a worthless plan.

In an IRS telephone scam, someone calls saying they are collecting a fine owed to the government and that they can reduce the fees if the amount is paid directly to them. The scam becomes real when the seniors pay via debit card or wire transfer.

To avoid being becoming a victim of telephone or telemarketing scams, seniors should not give any personal information, should request the offer in writing, and should not react quickly. They should check out unknown companies and research investments offered. Check companies through the Better Business Bureau and the National Fraud Information center. Beware of people claiming to be collecting money for a charity, for medical care, or for disaster relief.

- Do not allow anyone to pick up money from you for anything. You will never be able to find them again.

- Discuss possible ventures with close relatives or with a trusted financial advisor.

- Report any suspected fraud to local, state, and federal enforcement agencies. The Federal Trade Commission (FTC) website is https://www.ftccomplaintassistant.gov

Medicare, Medical Equipment, Medication, and Insurance Scams

A most challenging and anxiety arousing aspect of aging is health concerns. The preventative, diagnostic, and treatment aspects of a senior's health offer many opportunities for fraud and scams both of the senior and of government agencies.Between 60 and 80 billion dollars are lost due to Medicare fraud. It is fraud for anyone to steal a senior's Medicare benefits but this is not unheard of for this to happen when family members are having financial problems and have access to the senior's funds.

A current Medicare scam occurs when the scammer calls and says that new Medicare cards are going to be sent out and that they need to verify the senior's Medicare information. They request the senior's bank account information. Once they have this information, they have access to the senior's money. Be aware of this scam.

Another scam, sent out by email, is about the "new" June 13th Medicare Enrollment period. Actual open Medicare enrollment is between October and December.

Counterfeit medications, (which are dangerous) as well as a theft of an elderly person's money, are conducted mainly through the internet. Seniors search the internet to find better pricing for their medications. Counterfeit prescription medications will not help a person's medical condition but may actually do harm. Do not purchase medication from a vendor who does not require a doctor's prescription. Consult a pharmacist if medication packaging or appearance looks suspicious. Online prescriptions should have a seal of approval from The Verified Internet Pharmacy Practice Site. Many older Americans seek out anti-aging products and procedures in order to look younger. Thus they feel that they fit into the younger society better. Promotions for these products are seen on TV and on the internet with nomenclature such as "Secret Formula" and "Breakthrough Technique." These statements, as well as testimonials from celebrities, can be misleading.Treatment such as temporary facelifts, botox injections , and herbal internal and external applications are usually false and give large profits to an ever growing anti- aging industry. The danger in some of these treatments is that they can be administered or sold by charlatans with dangerous or even deadly consequences.Checking with the Better Business Bureau or with one's doctor is advised before taking any dietary supplements, signing up for any procedures, or taking any medications that could be potentially harmful or useless.

Another way of getting a senior's personal information is for the "vendor" to offer a "special" on medical equipment such as wheelchair, scooter, heart monitor, or even a tub seat. The "vendor" will request a mailing address, a deposit, and a way of billing (credit card, debit card). The equipment never comes but the money goes.

An extremely popular device for the elderly is the home alert system. While there are reputable and worthwhile systems they are never "free.".The vendors offering free medical alert systems find the senior through their vast automated dialing system which places thousands and thousands of calls a day. The senior is immediately instructed not to hang up and that they were referred to the vendor by the family physician or through the AARP. The senior is then directed to press a certain number on their telephone keypad which will record personal information and a credit card number. These pre- recorded messages are never legitimate. The recipient should just hang up and call local police. The FTC (1-888-382-1222) encourages seniors to call them to be placed on a "Do Not Call List"for these types of calls.

Health Insurance Frauds include over-billing of Medicare on forms that have counterfeit signatures, providers billing Medicare for services and procedures that were not performed, and fake tests given in malls and health clubs and then falsely submitted to insurance companies. Sometimes manufacturers will provide the senior with free medical equipment in exchange for their Medicare number, thus allowing them to falsely bill Medicare.

To avoid these scams seniors should not sign blank Medicare forms or do business with people offering free medical equipment. Seniors should review their monthly explanation of medical benefits notices to check what has been billed for against what services they were actually provided. Medical insurance information should only be given to those who provided medical services. They should also check what their copays are so that out of pocket expenses are known.

Internet Fraud.

The internet is THE way to obtain and communicate information. Not all seniors are as facile and comfortable with the internet as the younger generation. Thus they are more vulnerable to scam on the internet. They may open a pop up browser that promises anti- virus software only to find that in paying for it they have actually offered up personal information for abuse. Seniors can also open emails that appear to be legitimate (*i.e.* from the IRS) and respond to them and therefore reveal personal information.

They may order items on the internet, never receive the goods, but find their credit card information is used for other purposes.

Internet dating is often thought of as only for the young. But for senior widows, widowers, and those without a "significant other" it offers the senior hope of finding somebody to lessen the sense of being alone. Of the many internet dating sites that are deceptive, one of the most notorious is the Ghana romance scam. Here an individual , who eventually reveals that he lives in Ghana (or other African or Middle Eastern country), expresses an interest in finding a romantic partner and coming to the United States.

As the romance intensifies, the scammer makes requests for more and more reasons that he needs financial help, *e.g.* to acquire a visa, for a ticket to the US, for a medical problem, to clear up a debt. The reality of the person actually being a viable partner dwindles away as the scammer reveals himself through his poor grammar and idiosyncratic use of words not typical of a person of his supposed stature.

The June/July 2015 AARP magazine had an article titled "Are you Real?" The article follows the experience of a woman (Amy) who found herself alone after the death of her husband. Here is an abridged account of her story: Some time after her husband died Amy tried some dating sites. She truthfully filled out her profile for Match.com and was eventually matched with a 100% match (Dwayne). As their communication became more frequent, Dwayne became increasingly complimentary, sympatico, and professing strong romantic feelings for Amy. They progressed to phone calls during which Amy found herself very revealing to a man who was so interested in her. She found out little about him except that he traveled a lot, and sometimes was in Malaysia (which accounted for his phone calls at peculiar US times). They talked on the phone daily for hours.

Once she came home to flowers from him which had a very romantic note attached. Shortly after that, Dwayne revealed that due to a complication with his work he needed some money to cover some fees. First he needed $8,000, then $10,000. He knew Amy had the money because he knew that both her mother and husband had died and he knew she was in love. Eventually she lent him $100,000.

Then the contacts from Dwayne dwindled and then stopped. By that point she had already "lent" him $300,000. Shortly after that Amy spoke to an FBI agent.

It has been reported that many internet dating scammers are in fact based in Malaysia or Nigeria and that rarely are they found. Furthermore, at least some of the money they scam may be going to terrorist groups like Boko Haram in Nigeria. Suggestions for seniors considering online dating should NEVER share personal information.

Never send money. Report suspected scams to the FBI Internet Complaint Center. Do not keep in contact with someone who is not willing to meet with you within a month.

IRS Scams

The IRS contacts citizens by mail. All documents one needs for taxes (W-2s, mortgage statements, 1099s) should be received by March. The IRS rarely makes unsolicited phone call, faxes, or emails. Scammers send notices by fax and fake phone calls, claim to be from the IRS, and request personal and financial information. Sometimes scammers even rob mailboxes for notices that were actually sent by the IRS and then try to obtain a senior's money through illegal transfer of funds. Seniors who think that their mail was stolen should contact the IRS Identity Protection Unit at 1-800,908-4490, ext.245.

Scamming the Senior Homeowner

The second largest consumer complaint in the US , according to the Consumer Federation of America, are those related to home improvement and problems with contractors.

These scams, frequently on the elderly, include problems with overpricing, unfinished work, failure to have a written contract, poor workmanship, and work that does not meet building code requirements. These complaints are frequently the result of the person hiring a fraudulent worker. Seniors are an easy target for these crooks as they can no longer do repairs by themselves. In addition to dishonest home improvement offers, scams come via the internet, phone, and mail. These are inviting offers for home appliance, household repairs and warranties target unsuspecting seniors.

Phone rings (as I am typing this into my computer):

Dr. B. "Hello."

Caller: "Hello, how are you today. This is Jerry calling with GE Home Security."

Dr.B. "Tell me what your offer is." Caller hangs up.

Reverse Mortgage Scams

The number of reverse mortgages bought have increased more than 1,000 percent between 1999 and 2008.

Legitimate reverse mortgages or HECM loans are insured by the Federal Housing Authority. They allow homeowners to receive funds based on the equity they have in their home and thus avoid paying a monthly mortgage.Even legitimate reverse mortgages have their fees and specifications which should be carefully reviewed by the senior with input by a relative or someone else knowledgeable about the product.

Reverse mortgage scams are perpetrated by those who steal the home equity from an unsuspecting senior. Seniors who wish to obtain a reverse mortgage should seek their own mortgage consultant and ignore unsolicited advertisement on TV, radio, church bulletins, and investment seminars. They should not sign anything they do not understand .

Investment Scams

Seniors looking for ways to grow and safeguard their money have been a long-standing target for investment scams. These schemes are too numerous to describe but their commonality is that they often promise a lot and are too complex for the senior to understand. But they sound so reassuring and appealing. The pitch to be aware of is that the "investment" offers unrealistic big returns.

To avoid investment fraud:

- check out the "broker" on other websites.
- Do not respond to flashy websites.
- Do your homework to be sure about the company and be sure they are legitimate.
- Check out the "broker" on other websites.
- Do not invest with companies outside your own country.

Funeral/Cemetery Fraud

This is an easy one for scammers who read obituaries, attend the funeral, and find out information about the family there. Once getting the name they contact the grieving senior with false debt collection claims. They keep tremendous files on mourners to be used some time down the road on false dating sites, or "on the spot" contractor offering appraisals and discounts for home services.

Funeral assistance offers are an easy scam.The mailing addressed to A. Brandt "IS YOUR ADDRESS CORRECT?" offered by Lincoln Heritage Life Insurance Company guaranteed up to $20,000to the family in the event of my death, etc. ,etc. "MAIL TODAY! Requests received after 15 days may not be processed." All that was required was the return of the attached post card (to begin the scam).

Funeral home scams are easy to perpetrate on seniors who are typically overwhelmed. They do not have the time to read the fine print and follow the charges or procedures involved with the funeral. An example of this is the family who buys an expensive casket in which the loved one will be cremated — never to know that the cremation actually took place in a cardboard box.

Funeral homes charge fees for services and caskets. They are obliged to detail the costs over the phone or in person. Seniors should understand the fees when planning for their own funeral or that of a relative. They should contact several venders and read the entire contract before signing. They should also check cancellation options and the ability to switch to another funeral home if they move to another locale.

Seniors should apprise their family of their wishes and decisions. Do not allow funeral agents to pressure you into signing a contract.

The Grandparent Scam

This is an easy one because it preys on a grandparent's anxiety and emotional ties. It begins with the caller saying "Hi, grandma do you know who this is?" or, "Hi grandma. It's me."

The grandparent then easily provides the name. Remember the scammer only needs to get the response maybe one in fifty calls. The fake grandchild proceeds to play. "I'm in the hospital and don't have the moneyto pay the bill." or "I've been in an accident and don't have money to pay the bill. Please don't tell mom and dad. They would be so upset."

It's easy because all grandmas want to know is that that their grandchildren will be all right and sending a money gram or wiring the money by Western Union is the priority. Think of the information the scammer gets by this senior's transaction!

What should seniors do to avoid scams?

Start by being aware that there are an enormous number of scams, especially those directed at seniors. Go to the internet site https://www.fbi.gov/scams-safety/fraud . Read all the examples and read the suggestions there.

If your parent is a senior or if you are the senior, be in contact with family members to prepare for what to do in the event of suspected scam. There is no shame in being scammed or being approached by someone trying to rob you. Discuss how to report a scam to the authorities. This may protect others from the same scam. Try to figure out how the senior got on the scammers "hit list."

What is a senior's defense?

The cardinal thing for a senior to remember is NEVER Give out personal information (credit card numbers, bank account numbers, Social Security number, driver's license number) to Anyone.

A disturbing number of these scammers are not strangers. They are friends, relatives, neighbors, acquaintances.

In a study by MetLife it was reported that nearly $3 billion a year have been lost by seniors sixty and over.

AARP has developed a Fraud Watch Network which alerts seniors to new scams. Check in and sign up on your computer for scam alerts to:

http://www.aarp.org/money/scams-fraud/fraud-watch-network/

A new anti-fraud hotline launched by the Senate Aging Committee is 1-855-303-9470. Check businesses with The Better Business Bureau 1-703-276-0100.

- Be on guard for companies trying to do business from outside the United States.

- Understand exactly how any unsolicited offer works.

- Purchase merchandise only from reputable business.

- Make sure that venders have a valid business site and email address.

- Do not deal with anyone who pressures with "time limited offer" or "act now" offer.

- Do not do business with anyone who offers you a "free" anything which requires that you only pay shipping and handling, taxes, or a redemption fee in order to get the "free" gift.

Report suspected fraud to Fraud Hotline 1-800-222-4444, option 2 or AARP 1-800-627-2277.

Scammers throw out their bait to a large pool of thousands and thousands of seniors. They are very clever. Knowing who does and who does not respond and why, narrows their victims down to a list of most likely targets.

They hope to wean out the most astute and be left with the most gullible. Seniors should make sure they are crossed out , and therefore safe. Seniors must be alert and questioning, lest they become the bankroll for someone or something unscrupulous. Do Not Let Yourself be Scammed.

Chapter 11
THE HEALTHY SENIOR

Healthy ageing includes all aspects of life. It involves an understanding of the changes that come with ageing and an evaluation of one's physical, cognitive, social, emotional, spiritual, and purpose for being.

As life expectancy is increasing more seniors are taking care of themselves rather than being taken care of. More often now concerns with health become relevant in the late sixties or seventies. The eighties and nineties are now more often the time when physical and cognitive changes require outside help.

The senior years are not the time to be passive or lost. It is the time to accept who you are and not bemoan who you used to be. It is rather a time to decide how you will spend the remainder of your life.

This is so important a time of life that it should not be a rushing to fill time but rather should follow a pause, a quiet contemplative pause.

Sometimes senior-hood is misunderstood as a time to reinvent the self. In reality, who we are generally remains constant throughout our lives. Personality is formed at a very early age. While you can change aspects of your life, you are basically who you always were. Rather than reinventing the self, this is a time for knowing oneself and finding that which gives purpose and meaning.

This is also the time for realizing that life and time are indeed limited. One cannot move time backwards by looking and dressing or acting as one did at an early age. Ahead instead is the balance of your life and its finiteness becomes immeasurably valuable. The journey ahead is an opportunity to do what busy time did not permit before. There is no formula for these years but evaluating your past is a prerequisite for planning how to live the rest of your life. Accepting the wrong turns one has made allows you to move forward more positively. Understanding one's past does not mean wasting time being angry or remorseful. It means learning how to choose better and live more positively and purposely.

In all aspects of your life, use the lessons of the past to guide your future. Don't let doubt prevent you from moving forward. Ask yourself, ask others. Fine-tune your past or make changes. Make a plan. Nothing ever happens without a plan. Formulate a goal and be precise. What does it involve? Modify and reformulate when the plan is not working. Be realistic about how much you want the goal. What will help or hinder it being reached? Set down several options for obtaining your goal and chose the one with the highest chance of success.

Planning in your senior years requires will power and perseverance. Spend time thinking before you move. Listen to the voice inside you that will guide you to success in a way that fits who you are.

The Physical You: It is never too late to work towards a healthy lifestyle. Begin with easy changes and gradually move ahead. If you are ready for a real challenge use Dr. Dean Ornish's book *Dr. Dean Ornish Program for Reversing Heart Disease* (1996) as a guide.

Make sure you have a good primary care physician who knows you well and coordinates information from all of the medical specialists you see. Choose a primary care physician who is affiliated with the best hospital around.

Prevention at this stage of life becomes as important as treatment. Be sure to have health screenings, and do your own monitoring as to how you feel. Be an informed patient and have a central place where all your medical records are kept.

Be prepared for physical conditions that bring on pain. Pain is worse when you are alone. Doing something, getting out, talking to someone distracts from pain. Pain here, pain there. It is better to not let it run your life.

Diet: Changing to a healthy diet is something most of us have tried at least once. There are many challenging diets and exercise plans that are started and abandoned. Too much, too fast. Better to start with small steps and add to them. Eating healthy is important. It is disturbing to realize how many senior meals (especially of those who live alone) become bits of this and that, here and there, and smaller in quantity.

Perhaps decreased income, cooking for one, and preference for sweets, as taste buds for other foods become more blunted, contribute to poor diet in seniors. Poor diet though, results in poor health. The key to following a healthy diet is to find things that one really likes from each of the food groups. Find foods that provide you with necessary vitamins and minerals. If you find it difficult to keep track take a multivitamin pill to make sure you are meeting daily requirements. Experiment with fruits, vegetables, proteins that you have not eaten before. Incorporate foods you like. There is no use buying a "wonderful" health food if you don't like it.

- Eat three meals a day

- Start the day with a good breakfast, one high in protein and fiber, not carbohydrates

- Mommy was right. "Eat your vegetables" and fruit. Fresh fruit and vegetables (canned is ok if fresh is not available). are a good source of fiber, which is important to the mind and body as they start to slow down. Grains are also a good source of vitamins and fiber.

- Fill your protein requirements with less red meats and eat more lean meats. Eat baked, broiled, or poached fish. The omega 3 fatty acids in fish keep your heart and brain healthy.

- Eat foods that contain calcium (dairy and greens) to maintain healthy bones. Osteoporosis which occurs in men as well as women makes one susceptible to bone fractures. It is startling to see how many seniors begin the "slippery" slope to death subsequent to a severe bone fracture, especially the hip

    She was a feisty woman named **Hilda***. She was noted for being critical and complaining. Always positioned in her wheel chair in the same place around the nursing station where she could observe all the goings on.*

    The nurses asked the therapist to see her. She was a challenge but liked to talk and became less negative.

    One day she fell and broke her hip. Despite receiving care in the nursing home she began a very fast "slippery slope." What were the dynamics? Her fracture was no worse than others and she had good care.

    There is a mind body connection when it comes to broken hips. Perhaps it is related to the genetics of primitive nomadic tribes. When you can't keep up with the tribe your time is up. Hilda had no family or friends and no support system to convince her otherwise. The "slippery slope" ended in two weeks.

- Reduce your daily caffeine intake. Caffeine is not only found in coffee but in certain sodas, chocolate, and cold medicines. Caffeine affects both the heart and blood pressure and can affect the ability to fall asleep.

- Limit alcohol intake to one glass a day.

- Eat less fats, both in cooking and dairy products.

- Do not smoke. The proven deadly consequences of smoking are well documented. If you smoke, you must stop. Find a program. There are some that will help you stop.

Exercise: Physical exercise is anti-ageing. Move your legs, raise your arms, twinkle your fingers. Exercise keeps the blood moving thus providing nutrients and oxygen to all the organs. It has been shown to ward off anxiety and depression. Exercising, like healthy eating, will only succeed if you like what you are doing. There are many ways to get enough exercise. Finding a way that fits you may require some experimenting. Exercise can be done individually, in a group, indoors, outdoors, with friends, or in your own home. Exercise machines bought for the home have a high failure rate. Finding an exercise that is challenging and enjoyable increases the probability that it will be continued.

Any exercise program should begin gradually. Walking is the exercise of choice for seniors because it requires little equipment except for comfortable clothes and shoes. Walking tones the muscles, is good for the heart and lungs, and promotes a feeling of well-being. Aerobic walking, like any aerobic activity, improves mood by stimulating the productions of serotonin (a mood enhancing neurotransmitter in the brain).

If you have a hard time getting started, you must be creative. Here, for example, is how one gets to the gym. Small steps is the general recipe for success. First tell yourself to just put on your exercise clothes. This does not mean you have to go to the gym, but you put them on. Then tell yourself to go sit in the car. You don't have to drive just sit. But you will drive. After all you can just drive to the gym, sit outside, and then drive home. But you are in front of the gym. Well, you can just go to the lockers and come back. You need not go to the machines. But well you do some stretches and then just five minutes on the treadmill. Five minutes then just a quarter of a mile. Then fifteen minutes, then a half a mile, then twenty-five minutes, then a few more. Then there are the weights, some machines, change of pace, and then --- you have exercised.

Stimulating the mind: Sometimes we hear a senior say "I must be losing my mind." Meaning losing their cognitive abilities. While there is a typical slowing down of cognitive processes for some seniors, even small changes can be anxiety arousing.

In reality, the brain retains its mental functioning well into life. Barring some neurological disease the change that is most frequently observed is a slowing down of cognitive functions. But while it may take a bit longer to retrieve a bit of information it is important to know that the information is still there. It is not lost. Similarly while the speed at which new information is processed may slow down, the brain's ability to learn goes on and on.

Keeping the mind healthy requires stimulating the brain. Seniors should not only keep the mind active but more importantly challenge the brain in new ways. The brain has a tremendous capacity to learn and form new neural circuits and connections. Therefore trying something new enhances brain function.

In general, individuals tend to learn through a preferred modality. There are visual learners, people who learn by listening, and hands on learners. Recognize what kind of a learner you are and then try to learn using a different modality.

Stay current with what is happening in the world. Try to read a lot. Research has shown that people who read a lot stave off the effects of Alzheimer's longer than those who do not. Constant TV is boring. Substitute a new activity for TV. Mobile libraries provide an opportunity to obtain books and videos. Books on tape and books with large print are available to people with visual or hearing deficits.

Seniors need to appreciate the difference between being alive and having a life. Empty time is not fulfilling or mentally healthy.

Even for seniors living in a facility, the activities may not be the answer because they may fill time but do not fulfill the mind.

George Burns said "to get up in the morning and do something you love is the secret of long life. To find pleasure you must be willing to take a chance and make an effort."

Social Contacts: Nowadays, society is very mobile. If your family has moved around (as most do in these modern days) assess whether you are better off living where you are or moving to be close to your family. If possible live close to your family as it is likely that in time you will need to rely on them.

Have a support system of friends and relatives that you can talk to and depend on in times of stress. Try to expand this system by going to places where you will meet people with whom you can connect.

Social contacts are central to healthy ageing. Social isolation is a strong risk factor for poor health. Studies have shown that a senior's life style and environment are better predictors of risk for illness or mortality associated with ageing, than is a person's genetic makeup. Seniors who do not have a network of close relationships are at a higher risk. This underscores the need for seniors to maintain old, as well as make new, relationships. Intimate bonds with friends and family provide an opportunity for the reciprocal sharing of memories and feelings of closeness. A close confidant makes good things better and hard things easier.

Activities available to mobile seniors include travel groups, book clubs, restaurant clubs, political groups, or any group with whom they have similar interests. Homebound seniors can use the internet to keep in touch with family and friends.

Although it may be difficult to form new friendships and engage in new activities it is far more rewarding to take the steps to form social contacts than to be lonely and unconnected.

Physical intimacy –touch: In addition to social intimacy seniors need physical contact. The need for contact exists throughout life. Infants who do not receive enough physical contact suffer from a condition called "failure to thrive" in which their physical and psychological growth is thwarted. It is the rare individual, at any age, who does not benefit from physical contact. Families and caregivers who interact with a senior should be aware that a hug or a touch on the shoulder, benefits both the giver and the receiver. A massage, holding hands, and affection all help meet the need for touch.

The need for touch is the reason that pet therapy or having a pet is recommended for a senior. Holding and stroking a pet mitigates loneliness and provides comfort. Studies have shown that taking care of a pet gives a sense of satisfaction and purpose. Pet therapy has been used as an adjunct to the treatment of depression in the elderly.

Indulging and nurturing the body physically is restorative. A massage, mediation, sitting in the sun, sitting next to water, and listening to soothing music are examples of things that are calming and reduce stress. Sleep is the time the body replenishes itself. The mind and body are refreshed and restored during sleep. Poor sleep habits or sleep disorders disturb the normal sleep/wake cycle. Short term sleep disorders can result in anxiety, irritability, and fatigue the next day. Long term sleep disorders may put the senior at risk for depression, falls, and less efficient physical functioning. Good sleep is so vital for healthy mental and physical well-being that it is recommended that long term sleep disorders be managed with professional intervention.

Mood: As noted earlier, the changes experienced by a senior in transition make them vulnerable to mood disorders such as anxiety, depression, and adjustment disorder. Being physically, socially, and mentally healthy are good insurance against mood disorders as is having a positive attitude and being enthusiastic.

Being able to let go of past grudges and anger lowers stress. People with a good attitude don't spend their time worrying about getting old, being old, or dying. For them every day is a chance to be useful and to do something that makes them feel good.

An emotionally healthy person is one who welcomes the chance to share laughter. There are physiological mechanisms which connect laughter with the brain. Research has shown that laughter can be healing. It can reduce stress, mitigate pain, stimulate the body's immune system, and enhance mood. The connection between laughter and health is modulated through the brain's secretion of endorphin (the brain's pain killer), dopamine (the neurotransmitter that effects mood and motivation), and the decrease of a level of cortisol (the stress hormone in the body).

Despite one's best efforts to live positively it is important to recognize if one is experiencing a mood or adjustment disorder. These may require professional intervention from a geriatric psychologist or geriatric psychiatrist.

Make sure your primary care doctor knows the psychotropic medications you are taking and monitors them along with your other medications. Knowing how to enhance and maintain a positive mood is the foundation of a successful and healthy transition in the senior years.

Self-esteem and Purpose: Prior to retirement one's job is a major source of self-esteem and purpose. A job defines one's role and provides a frame of reference in society. Retirement changes this as well as changes finances and life style.

Men may feel especially less useful and may lose social contacts which were part of their job. Feelings of loss of power, uselessness, loss of identity, and lack of positive reinforcement from the job can affect self-esteem. In earlier stages of life, purpose and self-esteem came from work, family, teachers, spouses, and children. When one becomes a senior these references change. "All people when they are ageing want an opportunity to master things and challenge themselves. People want to do something meaningful and satisfying not just some mindless type of things." (US News and World Report. January 13, 2005 pg. 60.)

Individuals who looked forward to retirement may be surprised that it may feel more empty and purposeless than anticipated. Recreation is not enough. Seniors who are not actively engaged are likely to become sedentary. To be engaged is to be open to the world. This means being receptive to new information, opinions, and people who also increase awareness of what can be rewarding.

Finding a sense of purpose is a conscious, inward searching venture. It should follow a pause before asking such questions as: Who were you in the past? Who are you now? What are your talents, your gifts? What do you have to offer and how can you be productive? What do you expect of yourself rather than what do others expect of you?

Beyond purpose, seniors need to be treated with dignity and be empowered. This means staying involved in decisions and choices which affect your life. The importance of this is too often underestimated.

Passivity does not come easily to people who have made decision for themselves all their lives. It is not easy to give control to a caregiver. The giver of help is always more powerful than the receiver. It is therefore important for the senior to give back.

If seniors are encouraged to maintain independence for as long as possible and advocate for themselves, their self-esteem will not be compromised.

The Value of Seniors: People like to have seniors in their company just because they love them. To be with a senior is to have the opportunity to take part of the give and take of loving and there is nothing more valuable.

Seniors must not forget that they possess the wisdom and perspective that comes only with years of living. Data is what is here and now, what is current. Wisdom is knowing the big picture and having a type of learning and memory that gives an understanding of what matters. Wisdom, common sense, and intuition are a type of memory which involves storing up ideas that are made into connections in the brain. This memory is invaluable to problem solving. The longer one lives, the more such memories and connections are made in the brain. Seniors because of their longevity, excel in this type of memory. It does not fade with time. That is why a grandmother is consulted about a problem with a relationship. Although she may not remember all the details, her common sense and wisdom offer the best guidance. This wisdom enhances social intelligence which is why seniors have increased empathy. The wisdom of elders teaches us how to make a family and create a community. Their devotion instructs us in the acts of caring and giving, the most valuable lessons of life.

A senior possess the stories of your family. These stories about ancestors inspire and help families keep faith in times of trouble. We are connected to our past and our future through our place in time. Seniors connect us with our history through the knowledge of family stories.

It is hard to find a person, who throughout your life, wants to listen to the way a parent does. Even when they are elderly, your life has great importance to them and they are a source of love and caring. The value of their love and interest is enormous. It is a parent to whom you have listened, who has watched over you, and shared the memories of a lifetime.

Seniors need to be appreciated for their guidance, warmth, caring and the ability to go beyond themselves in times of need. When we get older ourselves we miss the conversations, the empathy, and the way our parents would comfort us when we were in need. Some lucky adult children can still hear the voices of their parent in times of need even when they are physically gone. Even when the mortal voice is still they can still stop and be silent and a parent's clear voice will speak to you from inside.

It is the old apple trees that are decked with the loveliest blossoms.

It is the ancient redwoods that rise to majestic heights.

It is the old violins that produce the richest tones.

It is the aged wine that tastes the sweetest.

It is the ancient coins, stamps, and furniture that people seek.

It is the old friends that are loved the best.

Thank God for the blessing of old age and the wisdom, patience, and maturity that go with it.

Old is wonderful.

Beautiful people are acts of nature it has been said.

But beautiful old people are works of art.

Sister Mary Gemma Brunke

Spirituality: Spirituality tends to increase with age. Many seniors find it important to have a sense of spiritual connection. For some this means an affiliation with an organized religion or religious observation, for others it is a personal relationship with God, or a life view and understanding of life's purpose. One does not necessarily go to a place of worship to nurture the soul and spirit. In fact as we age, the spirit is less easily crowded out by technology.

Finding your soul and spirit is a journey towards peace and tranquility. Find a place where you can be in touch with your inner self, with nature, and with a higher sense of holiness. Wend your way toward whatever your concept of holiness is. Pray from your heart. "A prayer is a plumb line, dropped to the center of the soul, a line to disclose your inner depths' (Wolpe, 1992, in Brandt, 1997). Wrap yourself in an idea of a God that feels comforting and is there with you when you reach out.

Chapter 12
AND AT THE END

Perhaps, it will make it (it being infinity) easier if you look up into the dark sky, sprinkled with sparkling stars and imagine that it goes on and on forever. Because what is there after forever? Well, outside of forever, there is another forever, and then infinite forever.

Then, in this cosmos of forevers, infinitely less than the most finite dot of time is you. There was of course a time, you remember, when you realized that you were not the center of the universe. That mind-altering moment, when perhaps your best friend said, "No, I don't want to play with dollies today, or your mother said, "When I have time, but you will have to wait". When that happy time in childhood development, diagnostically called the stage of narcissism, had to end. You looked around and saw that everyone thought that **they** were the center of the universe. And then we grow up and travel the train of life until the station is reached where we have to get off. Which brings us to "at the end".

Paradoxically, the first stage of life, birth, is the beginning of the journey towards death. We do not consider this concept when we watch a child grow and develop or when we see ourselves unchanged as we look in the mirror day by day. Even when confronted by an illness, or trauma, we expect to return to be as good as new.

With time, however, the body ages and is less able to restore itself completely. The baseline is reset. The goal, now, is to be as good as one can get.

This begins the last transition, a finality we cannot change. Different than other stages of life, where our choices and decisions determine outcome, the final outcome, now, is always the same. We are mortal and more certain than birth, is our death. Extended sometimes by medical intervention, the ultimate question remains "are you ready"?

Our cosmos is composed of stars and moons, and planets, and particles. Somewhere back, back, back, in time and space, on this earth, perhaps, guided by a higher power, the shifting and moving of atoms occurred in such a way that two particles kissed and conceived of the most primitive form of life. Evolving over, it is said, trillions of years into our now most complex of life forms, homo sapiens.

Unlike the infinity of the universe in which we dwell, life is finite. Regardless of its various complexities, all life - the antelope, the trees, the frogs, the rose, the eagle, the salmon that swim upstream to spawn, all have the commonality that they will die. And in fact, while alive, every living thing is here for the merest speck of time between one point and another. Finitely less than a nanosecond, in the specter of eternity.

The years of man are genetically programmed to last just so long. Survival of the fittest has made some changes in the life span in the animal as well as the human species, but not as much as we have been led to believe. Competition between males for the female has always existed. The strongest male tended to triumph and thus spread his seed, ensuring not only the survival of the species, but also of the fittest of the species.

Modern medicine has challenged Darwin's survival of the fittest by saving people from death and allowing, not necessarily the strongest or most capable to propagate, so we have "kindly" thrown a wrench into evolution and there is, perhaps, a moral/medical question.

The process which precedes death is a gradual deterioration of organs and systems programmed genetically to last that "finite time". In each person, some systems deteriorate more rapidly than others. This frequently is the underlying cause of a specific death. This programming is species-specific and necessary to preserve a balance in which the present generation must depart in order to make room for the next, hopefully more "fit' generation. "The race of man is like the race of leaves. As one generation flourishes, another decays… The preceding generation must yield space for the survival of the species (Homer).

Sherwin Nuland, in his book, *How We Die*, argues that modern medicine interferes with Darwinian laws of nature. He puts forth the idea that the medical model of saving lives has been guided more by the medical need to solve the problem (finding and fixing), thus prolonging life while disallowing graceful death.

The medical profession takes extreme exception to this proposition, acknowledging that, while they try to save lives, they oppose useless suffering, and costly, fruitless medical and technical interventions.

Advanced Directives do not always result in a tidy resolution of when someone dies. There are still times when it is questioned what qualifies as necessary as sufficient tubes, opiates, incisions, and machines. When has there been enough urging the body to continue, to work against the odds, in a painful and unnatural way? Who is served by the extra days or weeks, or even months of dis-ease, if the end is the same?

What is a good death? And what is an unnecessary death? Both may not be in control of the patient. There is death preceded by too much intervention and death preceded by too little intervention. There is death preceded by an unwillingness to let go on the part of the family and/or reluctance of the part of physicians who feel they must exhaust all options. The latter is an attempt to thwart death by searching for interventions that delay death as long as a flicker of life exists.

Too often, this inability to let go can compromise the comfort of the patient. Life in distress is prolonged without grace when the impossible supersedes the reality of a suffering patient. Knowing when to let go preserves the dignity of the patient and the medical team. In truth, the best one can hope for is to fulfill your dreams in that time between the start and finish, and to end that line with grace. Again, then, we ask, "What is a good death?"

People, who have had near death experiences, describe the closest thing that has been reported about death. What has been described is a sequence in which there is a separation from the body (perhaps it is the spirit or what is psychologically called the observing self). This part of the self is able to see the earthly organic body from a distance. This has been described as a peaceful (not anxious or depressing) process. This is followed by a passage through darkness and a perception of, and moving towards, light. Some individuals have reported having a life-review process proceed before them, and others feeling the presence of deceased loved ones.

So, if we take the reports as having some credibility, the death transition is not an unpleasant one. But this begs the question of a good death.

Most people do not think about the details of dying, even when they are quite advanced in age. No one ever prepares you for death or for the death of someone close — a friend, a relative — that painful twisting of your heart when a loss is near. Some people overreach to envelope and protect the vulnerable, others pull away because it reminds them of their own mortality. Most, if asked, would hope that death would come in a twinkle, like the blowing out of a candle. Thus, they can forestall the fear of an unpleasant, painful death. This, though, can lead them with no strategy, plan, or spiritual comfort when death is near. No comfort that after life they may really meet kindred souls in an afterlife. No reassurance of dying with dignity and peace. Thus one must face the fact that we often don't die in a way we would choose. Too often, it is prolonged discomfort due to deterioration and disease. So, hence, death is not necessarily merciful. In the best case scenario, the emotions of the dying and their families must be the priority. For this is a time of closure and of coming to terms with the things that were never done, the relationships that were never mended, the losses and grieving, the unrealized aspects of the self. A good death means letting go of everything that thwarts peace. For as hard as it may be, it is the only way to die with grace.

Most of all, people do not want to be alone when they die. So words of love, and praise, and sharing a good memory, would make one a lucky "dier." Just enough time for a gentle touch, a good joke shared, something soft on your skin, the last cool drop of ice cream on your tongue.

And a good death is knowing that you lived in the moment, immersed and aware of the things that served your senses. And knowing that you go on in the thoughts and memories of others who still can hear your voice. Relinquishing the narcissistic feeling that your death is a cosmic calamity, but instead aware of your oneness with an eternal unity in which everything has and had its place.

Epilogue
THEIR PRESENT IS OUR FUTURE

It should not surprise us if in many ways we will become much like our senior parents. After all, genetically, they passed on their DNA to us, and they raised us, thus influencing our values, beliefs, and behaviors.

As a corollary, this leads to the question of whether our senior transitions will be similar to our parents? Will we have their ailments? Will our children need to put us someplace? Will we feel lonely? Will we question our purpose?

There is a good chance that, at some time, you have caught yourself saying something, a special phrase or catch word that your parent said. Maybe you notice in yourself, the same mannerisms that were your parents. Perhaps someone tells you "you know now that you are older, you look just like your father". In the spring of 2006, actor Michael Douglas was a guest on a late night talk show. He had grown a beard for an upcoming movie role. He looked strikingly like his father, the venerated actor Kirk Douglas, when he was younger.

There are daughters who swear they will never be like their mothers. They are "superwomen," but they find that they revisit their mother's words and actions with their own daughters. "Put on a sweater." Is that all you're eating?" Daughters revisit aspects of their mother's personality, and in that way become like their mothers.

Sons take on their father's striving to achieve, their tendency to compete, or not compete. How often do you hear someone comment about their wives, "She's just like his mother"? It is likely that when we age, these similarities will crystallize, as will the idiosyncrasies.

198

Will we become outdated? Will we try to look young and embarrass our children? Will they want to include us in their world, even when our thinking falters, and when we need help getting around? Will they listen to our wishes? Will we still be able to make our choices? How often will we see our families? If we have to live in a facility, will someone come and take us out for the day?

Who will advocate for us – doctors, agencies or lawyers? Will they have time – everyone is always so busy?

Will we find ourselves in some of the stories in this book?

Who will care for us and tell us we matter? How will we matter? Who will take time and understand? Will we have Hope? Will we be ready?

BIBLIOGRAPHY

Bankson, Marjory Zoet. Creative Aging: Rethinking Retirement and Non-Retirement in a Changing World. *Vermont: Skylight Paths Publishing, 2010.*

Beauvoir, Simone de. The Coming of Age. *New York: G.P. Putnam's Sons, 1972.*

Brandt, Avrene. Caregiver's Reprieve. *California: Impact Publishers, 1997.*

Cullinone, Jon. The Single Woman's Guide to Retirement. *New Jersey: John Wiley & Sons, Inc., 2012.*

Feldesman, Walter. Long-Term Care at Home Consumer Guide. *New York: Walter Feldesman, 2009.*

Fox, Michael J. Always Looking Up. *New York: Hyperion Books, 2009.*

Frankl, V.E. Man's Search for Meaning, *Boston: Beacon Press, 1959.*

Goffman, Irving. Asylums: Essays on the Social Situation of Mental Patients and other Inmates.

Garden City: Doubleday and Company, Inc., 1961.

Kraetz, Eileen. A Spy in the Nursing Home. *Los Angeles: health Information Press, 1999.*

Holmes, T.H. and Rahe, R.H. Life Crisis and Disease Onset, I. Qualitative and Quantitative Definition of Life. Events Composing the Life Crisis. *Submitted to* Psychosomatic Medicine, *1996.*

Linkletter, Art. Old Age is Not for Sissies. *New York: Viking, 1988.*

Lustbader, Wendy. Counting on Kindness: The Dilemmas of Dependency. *New York: The Free Press, 1991.*

Maitz, Sandra (Editor). When I am an Old Woman I Shall Wear Purple. *California: Papier-Mache Press, 1987.*

Morse, Sarah and Robbins, Donna Quinn. Moving Mom and Dad! *CA: Lanier Publishing, 1998.*

Nuland, Sherwin B. How We Die: Reflections of Life's Final Chapter. *New York: Alfred A. Knopf, 1993.*

O'Brien, Mary, M.D. Successful Aging. *California: Biomed General, 2007.*

Ornish, Dean, M.D. Dr. Dean Ornish Program for Reversing Heart Disease: The Only System Scientifically Proven to Reverse Heart Disease without Drugs or Surgery. *Joy Books, Ballantine Books, NY, 1996.*

Pierskalla, Carol and Heald, Jane. Help for Families of the Aging. *Swarthmore, PA: Support Source, 1992.*

Reichel, William (Editor Emeritus) Reichel's Care of the Elderly. Clinical Aspects of Aging. *5th Ed., Baltimore: Lippincott, Williams and Wilkins, 1999.*

Roiter, Bill. Beyond Work. *Ontario: John Wiley & Sons, 2008.*

Romano, Joseph L. Legal Rights of the Seriously Ill and Injured: A Family Guide. *PA: Joseph L. Romano, Esq., 2011.*

Simpson, Carol. At the Heart of Alzheimer's. *Gaithersburg, M.D: Manor Healthcare Corp., 1996.*

Thayer, Jane and Thayer, Peggy. Elder Essence: The Gift of Longevity. *Maryland: Hamilton Books, 2005.*

Index

www.ingramcontent.com/pod-product-compliance
Lightning Source LLC
Chambersburg PA
CBHW072133270326
41931CB00010B/1748